BETTER BIBLE STUDY

A. Berkeley Mickelsen
and
Alvera M. Mickelsen

G/L
REGAL
BOOKS
™

A Division of G/L Publications
Glendale, California, U.S.A.

Other good Regal reading on related subjects:
A Look at the New Testament, Henrietta C. Mears
A Look at the Old Testament, Henrietta C. Mears
Understanding the Bible, John R.W. Stott
B.C., A Digest of the Old Testament,
    John Calvin Reid, Compiler
Handbook of Bible Lands, Guy P. Duffield
The New Testament in Living Pictures,
    David S. Alexander
The Old Testament in Living Pictures,
    David S. Alexander

The Scripture quotations in this publication unless otherwise
indicated are from the *Revised Standard Version*, copyrighted
1946 and 1952 by the Division of Christian Education of the
NCCC in the U.S.A., and used by permission. Others are:
The authors' literal translation.
KJV Authorized *King James Version*.
NEB From *The New English Bible, New Testament.* © The Delegates
of the Oxford University Press and the Syndics of the Cambridge
University Press 1961, 1970. Reprinted by permission.
ASV American Standard Version, 1901.
NASB New American Standard Bible. © The Lockman Foundation,
1971. Used by permission.
Phillips The New Testament in Modern English, copyright J.B.
Phillips 1958. Used by permission of the Macmillan Company.

Published by
Regal Books Division, G/L Publications
Glendale, California 91209, U.S.A.
Printed in U.S.A.

Library of Congress Catalog Card No. 74-32327
ISBN 0-8307-0358-6

CONTENTS

PREFACE

The science of interpreting the Bible, known as hermeneutics, has become increasingly important during the last decades and now enjoys an important place in the study courses of most theological seminaries and in some Bible colleges. For this we are thankful.

But the questions involved in determining what the Bible means are no longer limited to the pastor and the scholar. With the growing emphasis on the role of lay people in the church, every Christian finds it necessary to interpret the Bible.

This volume is dedicated to helping each Christian to understand the Bible better and to helping others meet God in its pages.

Much of the material for this volume is based on *Interpreting the Bible*, published in 1963. It has been used primarily as a textbook in seminaries, colleges, and departments of religion in universities. This shorter volume is geared to the person who knows little or nothing about Greek or Hebrew and whose background in contemporary philosophy is limited. A more complete discussion of most of the subjects included in this book may be found in *Interpreting the Bible*, Wm. B. Eerdmans Publishing Company, Grand Rapids, Michigan.

A. Berkeley & Alvera M. Mickelsen
St. Paul, Minnesota, 1976

INTRODUCTION

This book has one purpose—to help the reader learn how to discover what the Bible means. Why do we need a book to tell us that? Why not just read the Bible and see for ourselves what it says and means? We can and should. But we may need some help in doing so.

Most of the books we read have been written during our generation for the people of our day. The writers share much of their readers' cultural background and most of the familiar current thought patterns. When this is not true, we find a book hard to read.

Most people who pick up this book will not have a reading background in Oriental philosophy. Such books are available, but even though they have been translated into our language—into words that we recognize—they are often hard to read because the total framework of thought is strange to us. We are not comfortable in it.

When today's readers struggle through Greek mythology or Beowulf, or even Shakespeare, they must be constantly interpreting them. The words are the words of our language, but the setting is strange. The people think differently than we do. They often have a different set of values. Even though we may recognize certain universal themes that are common to us in our day, we must make the transition from another culture and time to our own, if the message is to be relevant.

The same is true of the Bible. It was written in a period roughly 2000 to 3000 years ago, in different languages and for people whose thought patterns, customs and ways of life were very different from ours. The writers of the Bible were part of their generation just as we are part of our generation.

In studying the Bible, we are always confronted with the questions: What did this mean to the original readers? What does it mean to the readers today? In answering these questions, we are in the process of interpreting the Bible.

The Bible is by no means the only document that must be so studied to be understood. Volumes have been written interpreting Plato, Aristotle, and Kant. The archaeologist who analyzes the Dead Sea Scrolls must use every sound principle and skill at his command to determine what the writings mean.

Perhaps the classic example of a document that must be studied to be understood is the Constitution of the United States. Throughout the history of this nation, the justices of the Supreme Court have given their full time to interpreting what the Constitution of the United States meant when it was written and what it actually means today. Yet that document was prepared in English, only 200 years ago.

It is especially important that we use great care in interpreting the Bible, for we are dealing with material of infinite worth—the very message and revelation of God. To the Christian, the Bible is the guidebook for all of life. It shows us the way to fellowship with God. It teaches what God expects of men and women. It is the one great record of God's fullest revelation of Himself in the person of Jesus Christ. Since fellowship with God is indispensable for a satisfying life, we dare not jeopardize it by a faulty reading or understanding of the Bible.

Incorrect interpretations of the Bible have had terrible results in days past. Erroneous interpretations have been used to support wretched causes, including racial discriminaton, slavery, and particular views of science. One of the blackest chapters in Christendom appeared in the seventeenth century when the great mathematician Galileo was tried and convicted by his church for propounding the Copernican theory that the earth revolved around the sun as against the "scriptural" view that the earth was the center of the universe.

Why have such things happened? Because honest, conscientious people *confused the message of God with their interpretation* of the words of the Bible. The two are not synonymous, and it takes an honest person to admit that some of his deep convictions (often held with the most intense emotion) are based on a particular interpretation of certain verses of the Bible rather than on the basic message of God given in the Bible.

This is the problem that all Christians face. This volume will not give you a one-two-three formula guaranteed to bring "instant understanding" to difficult passages, but it will give some basic principles to guide your own thinking and to help you weigh the interpretations that you hear and read.

How to Use This Book

Look up the Scripture references when the passage is

not quoted in full. Only then can you practice what you are learning while you read this volume. Scripture passages are usually quoted from the *Revised Standard Version.* In some instances, particularly in the chapter on poetry in the Bible, a more literal translation from the original languages may be given. It is often wise to compare several translations of the passage you are studying.

Make use of the Index to Scriptures in the back of the book. It lists every Bible passage that is referred to or discussed in this book.

Study and read critically. You will experience a new exhilaration as you learn to make your own judgments based on firm principles, and the Bible will become more alive and powerful in your life. Remember, God intends for you to *understand* this remarkable book, and to meet Him in its pages.

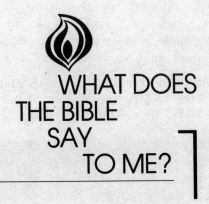

WHAT DOES THE BIBLE SAY TO ME?

The Bible is not a book of magic. It does not give the reader instant right answers to difficult questions nor a foolproof green or red light on decisions he must make. But most people who make a practice of daily Bible study do find that it helps them to have fellowship with God, renews them for the demands of the day, and provides moral guidance for daily conduct.

We are usually benefited by reading the Bible, even if we do it poorly. Unquestionably, to read the Bible poorly and with little understanding of good methods of interpreting is better than not reading it at all. It is also better to eat a poor diet than to starve to death! But a healthy body demands a healthy diet and a healthy spiritual life demands good Bible study practices and principles.

The basic principles of sound interpretation are just as important for the Christian in his personal devotional Bible reading as they are for the professional Bible teacher or pastor. All sound Bible study demands that we ask two questions of every passage:

1. What did it mean to the first hearers or readers?

2. What does it mean to me and other Christians of my time?

The questions need to be asked in that order, for understanding what a passage meant to the first reader or hearer will often keep us from reading our own ideas into the words of Scripture. To know what it meant to the first reader or hearer often demands that we know something of the history and culture of the people to whom the message first came. This aspect is discussed at length in chapter 6.

Does this mean that the average Christian cannot profit from personal Bible reading unless he consults scholarly tools at every verse? By no means. The Holy Spirit has promised to enlighten us. "When the Spirit of truth comes, he will guide you into all the truth" (John 16:13). Jesus' words quoted in John were spoken to His disciples at the Last Supper, and since every believer is a disciple in a broader sense (see Matt. 28:19), this passage is also applicable to us. However, the assurance of the Holy Spirit's presence as a teacher does not mean that Christians can use haphazard study methods and justify any conclusion they reach by saying, "God told me this in my Bible reading."

If we consider the Bible to be sacred and crucial to our spiritual growth, we must be extra careful to avoid poor study methods and erroneous conclusions.

What *can* we expect from devotional study? Most of us know that we cannot expect our Bible reading to provide answers to such specific questions as "Shall I change from this job to that one?" But do we know what we can rightly expect from personal devotional reading of the Bible? We can expect at least three results from conscientious Bible study: *God speaks to us through Bible study; God guides our decisions through Bible study; God helps us grow through Bible study.*

11

God Speaks to Us Through Bible Study

We say that when we pray we speak to God; when we study the Bible God speaks to us. This is true if we understand what is meant by "God speaks to us" during our devotional reading. How can we know God is speaking to us?

There are two variables in our personal Bible study. First, the passage we read will change from day to day—we seldom read the same chapters and verses day after day; second, our own needs change from day to day. How God speaks to us during our Bible study will depend on the passage we read and our own needs on that day.

Suppose you are reading in Philippians and you come to chapter 4, verses 2,3. Paul addresses two women, Euodia and Syntyche, pleading that they live in harmony in the Lord. He praised the two as those who "have fought at my side in [spreading] the gospel." Paul also encouraged an unnamed individual whom he calls "true yokefellow" to help these two women who were quarreling. What can this legitimately say to us? How can God speak to us through this passage?

First, *we must examine the context of the passage— what comes before and after this section.* The letter to Philippians is short enough to read easily in a single sitting. When we do so we find that Paul is writing to a church for whom he has great affection. He experiences joy and thanksgiving when he thinks about this group of Christians. It is the only church from whom Paul accepted gifts (see Phil. 4:15,16). The letter is full of profound ideas which Paul apparently thought these believers were able to understand and accept.

However, the verses about Euodia and Syntyche are introduced without any stated reason for the disagreement between these two women. We do not know the

12

cause of their quarrel nor how "true yokefellow" fits into the picture.

So next *we must look for certain principles of action* revealed by the passage. Several principles emerge from these two verses: First, believers ought to live in harmony and love toward one another; second, if there is a quarrel within the family of God, a third person may need to try to help resolve the problem; and third, Paul considered the work of these women, "his fellow laborers" (persons engaged in the same contest), to be important in the church. These women are mentioned on the same level with Clement and the rest of Paul's fellow workers. (See Phil. 4:3; Rom. 16:3; Phil. 2:25; Philem. 24.)

What will stand out to the individual reader may depend on what is his personal situation and need. But each of these applications is a *principle* that came from the passage and anyone who belongs to God can apply the principles if he finds himself in a situation where they are relevant.

We must distinguish between history and instruction as God speaks to us in our Bible study.

When Judas found that he had sold Jesus into the hands of His enemies and that Jesus was going to die as a result, his remorse was so great that he went and hanged himself. Does that mean if a Christian does some great sin, he should do likewise? Obviously not.

In the account of Judas, the Bible is faithfully recording events that took place. It is in no way giving an example to be followed.

The same may be true in other passages that are not so obvious. In Acts 4:32–37, there is an account of the early Church in Jerusalem, telling that the early Christians voluntarily sold what they possessed and brought the money to the apostles for distribution as each had

13

need. Does this mean that private property is to be abolished among Christians? Some have thought so. But again, the passage does not present this as an instruction to Christians. It simply tells what one group of early believers did.

However, the New Testament does give some specific instructions about feeding the hungry: "If a brother or sister is ill-clad and in lack of daily food, and one of you says to them, 'Go in peace, be warmed and filled,' without giving them the things needed for the body, what does it profit? So faith by itself, if it has no works, is dead" (Jas. 2:15–17).

We must recognize differences in culture. Some commands are for a particular person in a particular situation. Although Timothy is encouraged to take a little wine for the sake of his stomach and his other frequent ailments (see 1 Tim. 5:23), the modern reader who also may have stomach troubles cannot take this as a divine prescription for his own physical ills.

Throughout the Bible there are commands for specific persons and specific situations. The question often arises as to whether those commands apply to all persons and all situations. An understanding of the historical and cultural background often clears up the questions.

Paul's letters were written to specific churches with particular problems. For example, in 1 Corinthians 14:35, Paul writes, "It is shameful for a woman to speak in church." Is this a universal teaching?

The context of this verse indicates that Paul was trying to help the Corinthians restore order in their church gatherings. A study of culture shows that most Gentile women of that day were illiterate and Jewish women believers had no instruction in the Old Testament because rabbinical tradition forbade their being taught.

In the synagogue and in the early Church, it was the custom for one person to read the Scriptures, perhaps speak, and for men of the congregation to interrupt with questions as they chose. The women of the Corinthian church were far behind the men in their religious understanding because of the culture of their area, so Paul told them to save their questions until they got home and then ask their husbands. Would Paul say the same thing to women in American churches?

Actually, we know Paul did not really mean "silence" even in Corinth because in 1 Corinthians 11:5 (also discussing order in services) he gives instruction as to *how* women are to prophesy in the meetings—with their heads covered. Paul's instruction might be based on the custom of that day that married women wore veils. Or it might refer to a special hairstyle for women who were prophets.

Specific commands of the Bible often need a study of culture and historical situation to understand their significance. But we must not stop at this study. We must take what God has revealed to us and apply it to our daily lives.

God Guides Our Decisions Through Bible Study

Every believer who takes his faith seriously soon finds that all his decisions must be God-centered. We must make decisions each day of our lives. Sometimes the decisions seem small at the time, but weeks or years later we may find that a seemingly unimportant decision had far-reaching results.

What role can our Bible reading play in these minor and major decisions?

The Bible often provides us with definite principles that can help us make decisions. A man on the verge of getting involved in an extramarital affair need not search far in the Bible to find the principles that tell him "No" in clear terms—if he is willing to see them. The same goes for business dealings that have dishonest angles, or that exploit people. The Old and New Testaments are full of warnings of the judgment of God on such activity. But not all decisions are so black and white.

On some occasions the believer must seek broad principles in making decisions. In some instances, if we know God's will for other individuals, we may rightly conclude that our situation is parallel and that this is God's will for us.

For example, a Christian may become ill of a chronic disease such as heart trouble, arthritis, diabetes, or asthma. He makes use of all the help God has provided through modern medicine. He and his friends pray earnestly for healing and deliverance from the disease. He seeks to live to please God. If God does not grant healing, that person may conclude as he reads 2 Corinthians 12:7–10, that God's will for him is like God's will for Paul—"My grace is sufficient for you, for my power is made perfect in weakness."

A closer study of the passage shows that Paul felt that his affliction came to him because of the abundance of revelation he had received from God. In this sense, Paul's experience is no doubt different from ours. Yet Christians throughout the years have experienced God's power energizing and strengthening them in physical afflictions and have learned to say with Paul, "I will all the more gladly boast of my weaknesses, that the power of Christ may rest upon me" (2 Cor. 12:9).

Christians sometimes want specific commands on subjects that the Bible does not discuss. What does the Bible say about scuba diving? Nothing, of course. How then can the Christian know whether it is God's will for him to take up scuba diving? The principles of time or money involved, the aftereffects on the Christian's interest in the things of God, the help or hindrance in testifying for God, the effect on the physical and emotional well-being of himself and his family—each of these principles will help the individual Christian to make a decision.

One person might find that scuba diving takes too much time. Another might find that the exhilaration that follows gives greater efficiency in his or her work for God, and that it is a good thing. We need not fear leaving such decisions in the hands of the individual believer who honestly seeks the mind of God in all matters. We are to "test everything; hold fast what is [morally] good" (1 Thess. 5:21).

Even in major decisions, such as choosing a life partner or choosing a lifework, you will not find specific answers in the Bible. However, the conscientious student will find principles to help him make decisions. The Bible says much about the attitudes of husband and wife toward each other and toward God. Marriage is to be "in the Lord" and it is to be a holy relationship. They are to submit themselves "one to another." (See Eph. 5:21; 1 Cor. 7:39; 1 Thess. 4:1–8.)

Regarding a life vocation, Paul stresses the importance of work and that whatever a believer does, he is to bring glory to God. (See 2 Thess. 3:10,12; 1 Cor. 10:31.) The more familiar we are with the Bible, the better will be our understanding of the principles it teaches and how they bear upon our daily lives.

But is that all there is to "guidance from God"? No, there are other factors too.

Guidance involves a self or personality centered on God. If our lives revolve primarily around ourselves, we can hardly obtain guidance from God. God is not like

17

a tax consultant whose services are sought when things get too complicated. We cannot ask God to straighten out our problems unless we also want Him to straighten out our lives.

Guidance includes an awareness of how events and past experiences have prepared the way for the present. How did we come into our present situation? Was it by seeking God, or by seeking what we wanted?

If we want God's guidance, our prayer life must demonstrate a complete openness to God. Paul's prayers were nearly all contingent on "if God is willing" (see Rom. 15:32). Prayer is hard work because we must put all that we are into the experience.

In seeking God's guidance a person must develop a quiet dependence on the Holy Spirit to illumine his or her understanding.

The person who is centered upon God has a better perspective on the alternatives facing him in his decisions, knowing that God has directed his steps in the past. Guidance involves the courage to act with confidence in God.

God Helps Us to Grow Through Bible Study

The Bible gives many commands that touch every aspect of our lives. When we obey these commands we will grow in our spiritual life.

First Thessalonians 5:12–22 is one passage that speaks to us on an amazing variety of subjects:

1. Esteem for spiritual leaders (vv. 12,13).
2. Group harmony—"Be at peace among yourselves" (v. 13).
3. Lazy people—"Admonish the idle" (v. 14).
4. Discouraged people—"Encourage the fainthearted" (v. 14).
5. Morally weak people—"Help the weak" (v. 14).

6. Attitude toward people—"Be patient with them all" (v. 14).

7. Retaliation—"See that none of you repays evil for evil" (v. 15).

8. Good works—"Always seek to do good to one another and to all" (v. 15).

9. Optimism—"Rejoice always" (v. 16).

10. Prayer—"Pray constantly" (v. 17).

11. Thankful spirit—"Give thanks in all circumstances; for this is the will of God in Christ Jesus for you" (v. 18).

12. Holy Spirit—"Do not quench the Spirit" (v. 19).

13. Prophecy—"Do not despise prophesying" (v. 20).

14. Discernment—"Test everything; hold fast what is good" (v. 21).

15. Evil—"Abstain from every form of evil" (v. 22).

Each of these commands can give us help in our daily living and decision making. However, merely reading and understanding God's instructions to us is not enough.

We must spend time meditating on what we read in the Bible. In Western society, we are not in the habit of meditating. We would rather read someone else's comments on a Scripture verse, or memorize it, or trace down similar passages—almost anything in preference to the hard work of thinking for ourselves about what this means and where it fits into our own lives.

Many Christians are helped by applying four questions to their daily Bible reading. Ask, "What in this passage applies to:

1. my relationship to God?

2. my relationships to other believers?

3. my relationship to those who have no fellowship with God?

4. my responsibility for myself—my personal outlook, attitude, growth, temptations, desire for maturity in Christ?"

Spending time meditating on God's Word helps us to grow spiritually.

We must share what God reveals to us. Christ clearly taught that the believer is to be a witness for Him "in Jerusalem and in all Judea and Samaria and to the end of the earth" (Acts 1:8).

We are to help one another—to encourage, comfort, give help as needed. We are also to reach out to unbelievers with the redeeming message of Christ. We are to use the Bible in personal dialogue. What is the role of the Bible in this?

The Bible is our most important means for knowing God and discerning His will for us. But that does not mean that Christians are to go through life quoting verses of the Bible at every turn to each person with whom they have contact. This is usually a lost cause because most non-Christians have little or no understanding of the concepts of the Bible. And unless a modern speech version is used, they may not even understand the words spoken.

The most important factor for Christians to remember when they minister through personal dialogue is that they must *listen* as well as speak. Dialogue means *two* people talking. Too often we think *we* are to talk while he or she is to listen. Unless there is honest listening and a real attempt at understanding why other persons feel and think as they do, little is accomplished. But when we have honestly listened and sought to understand, then we can choose, with the help of the Holy Spirit, the right biblical idea and passage to help the individual.

The more we understand the Bible in its original setting and to its original readers, the easier it is for us to recognize the teachings and principles that can help us in our situations and those of our friends.

The hallmark of the early Christians was their love for one another. Where there is true love, there is more likely to be true listening. Both participants will listen to what God is saying through the Scriptures and both will sense the presence and power of God.

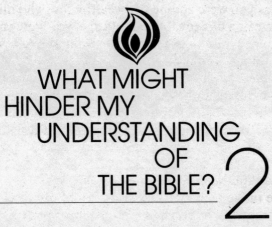

WHAT MIGHT HINDER MY UNDERSTANDING OF THE BIBLE? 2

Most people begin reading and studying the Bible with a sincere desire to know what it says and teaches. But none of us comes to the Bible neutral. We have all been previously and unconsciously conditioned, and this preconditioning either helps or hinders our ability to learn.

Our Culture Conditions Our Understanding

We have been conditioned by the culture in which we live. To most of us, bread means a loaf we buy at the supermarket. Home means a comfortable house or apartment. Travel means a trip by car, plane, bus, or train. Old age means a period of retirement when a man is free to pursue his own interests if his health permits.

Yet these concepts are largely limited to the middle-class American who lives in the last half of the twentieth century. They were unknown to the times during which the Bible was written. In Bible times, bread was the staple of life—baked in your own primitive oven from grain you grew, harvested, and ground yourself. Home usually involved shelter for your family and your animals—sheep, oxen, etc. Travel involved a long trek by foot unless you were among the wealthy few who might ride a horse or a donkey. In your old age, you were cared for by your children—if you were among the few who lived to old age.

The Bible comes alive to us more and more as we begin to understand the culture and historical situation in which it was written. We must journey to its culture rather than trying to impose our thought patterns and life-styles on the Scriptures.

The "Scientific Method" Influences Us

We are influenced by the philosophy of the world in which we live. Part of this philosophy involves the "scientific method" that is built on a cause-effect relationship and demands that almost every aspect of life be in some way measurable. Our world is one in which imagination is dedicated mostly to the material aspect and the pursuit of more and better things.

However, the principles of logic or research that may be applicable to the study of sciences or even of the humanities often are not applicable to the biblical sphere. But this we are reluctant to accept, for the pressures of a "cause and effect" universe bear down on us. We think we must find an explanation for every miracle, for every bit of predictive prophecy that was fulfilled. Our conditioning makes it difficult to deal with biblical materials within the framework of their day rather than our own.

Early Religious Beliefs Bias Us

We are conditioned strongly by the religious beliefs (or lack of them) with which we grew up. Ideas planted early are hard to root out—whether they are good or bad. We find that none of us comes to the Bible with a truly open mind. Our preconceived notions condition the way we interpret the Bible.

Some of this conditioning may involve concepts that are foreign to the Bible and hinder our understanding of its meaning. For example, some people *assume* (because they have been told so) that later religious ideas are always more fully developed than earlier ones. If this is their assumption, they will find in earlier writings ideas to prove that the God of the Jews is a tribal deity among the other tribal deities of other groups. They then look for evidence of a developing concept of one supreme universal God. Because they are looking for this, they tend to overlook anything that does not fit into this pattern and to pounce on every shred of information that would support their idea. Yet the biblical emphasis is on the tendency of men to wander away from God—not to grope toward Him! Religious ideas during periods of revolt against God are not necessarily more developed than the earlier ideas that were expressed when genuine faith and commitment were present.

We are all tempted to twist the Bible into the shape that pleases us and to make it say what we want it to say. Sometimes this can reach alarming proportions. For example, some have insisted that the Greek word *apostasia* (meaning apostasy), that is translated "falling away" in the *King James Version* and "rebellion" in the *Revised Standard Version*, actually means "rapture" in 2 Thess. 2:3. "For that day will not come, unless the rebellion comes first, and the man of lawlessness is revealed, the son of perdition." Making *apostasia* into

24

"rapture" instead of "rebellion" is defended by a complicated appeal to etymology (root meaning of words); however, there is no support for any meaning other than "apostasy" or "rebellion" among writers of koine Greek during the period in which the New Testament was written. The effort to find "rapture" in that word is made to support a particular theological viewpoint.

Paradox Confounds Us

Our preconceived notions and ideas often get us into trouble in understanding the Bible because we are used to systematic thought patterns. We want a well-ordered theological or philosophical point of view. Some statements in the Bible seem to be paradoxical and since our minds find it hard to tolerate paradox, we ignore one idea and exalt another when we come to ideas that cannot easily be reconciled.

This is especially true when we become enamored with some minor element of the Bible and then try to see that element everywhere. We can turn almost any passage into support for our favorite theme. When we do this, we have lost our sense of balance. Under the illusion of being exhaustive in our study, we find support for our idea in places where a normal reading of the passage (remembering the original readers' situation) would give an entirely different meaning.

Unfortunately some such assumptions have been widely popularized. The average reader or hearer never bothers to look up the context of all passages by which the writer or speaker has "supported" his case. Thus he may not realize how much may have been taken out of context and misused.

Our Intense Individualism Hinders Us

American society is strongly geared to individual interest and progress. We pride ourselves on the idea that every individual is judged on his own merit, regardless of his or her background, family, education, race, creed, etc.

But the Bible did not rise out of that kind of society. In the Old Testament, the individual was dependent for his very existence on his family and tribe. The *group* to which a person belonged was rewarded or judged.

When Achan disobeyed God (Josh. 7) and kept some of the artifacts from Jericho, not only was he slain, but also his sons, daughters, oxen, asses, and sheep. This seems incomprehensible to us in our individualistic society, but it flowed naturally from the structure of the group culture of that day.

We cannot impose our twentieth-century society patterns on the Bible nor sit in judgment when it does not conform to our pattern.

Our Own Dogmatic Attitude Limits Us

We tend to assume that there is only one possible meaning for a particular passage—*our* meaning! Often the language is such that more than one interpretation is genuinely possible and we should resist the temptation of insisting that if ours is possible, all other are impossible.

Being aware of the pitfalls that easily ensnare us will help us to recognize our own tendencies and seek God's help in overcoming them.

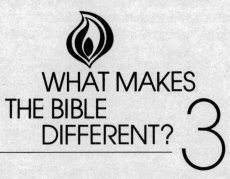

WHAT MAKES THE BIBLE DIFFERENT? 3

The Bible is a unique book! Though there are many ways in which it differs from other "religious" books, all these pale into insignificance before one overwhelming conclusion: This is a book with a message, a message that meets the basic need of man. And what is this message? It is twofold: *God desires fellowship with man and God has provided the means by which such fellowship is possible.*

Four other characteristics also make the Bible different from other books: (1) its authority, (2) its unity, (3) its diversity and (4) its inspiration.

The Bible Claims Authority from God

The authority of the Bible is no other than Jehovah Himself. Jehovah is the God who acts. He is also the God who speaks. And throughout the Old Testament, the writers insist that Jehovah speaks—to the prophet, to the king, to the priest or to the people. Four basic words or phrases in Hebrew declare that God has something to say.

The Old Testament uses several variations of the expression *neum*, having to do with the utterance or declaration of Jehovah: "the utterance of Jehovah of hosts"; "the utterance of the Lord Jehovah"; "the utterance of the Lord, Jehovah of Hosts" and "the utterance of the King whose name is Jehovah of Hosts."

This term "utterance" in reference to God appears 366 times in the Old Testament and most often in the prophets—more than 100 times in Jeremiah alone, and 85 times in Ezekiel. And each time the expression is used, the context stresses that the declaration is made by the God who has entered with a note of authority, as men are called to hear what God has to say to them.

There are also several variations of the expression *amar* involving the word "to speak." This word usually appears in phrases like, "thus says Jehovah, the God of Israel"; "thus said the high and lofty one"; "thus saith the Lord Jehovah and thy God," etc.

These expressions or some variation of them appear 436 times in the Old Testament. Sometimes they involve judgment, sometimes blessing. Often Israel disregarded the messages, but they were still preserved in the Old Testament to remind future generations of God's claim upon His people and their position under the authority of God.

The common Hebrew word *davar* also means "speak." This verb is often used of ordinary speech. It is also used frequently when the subject is Jehovah, God, Lord, Spirit of Jehovah, etc. Again the implication is that God is present among His people in judgment or in blessing.

Davar appears 525 times in the Old Testament. In the passages using this term, God communicates to His people through His chosen messengers in such a way that those who really listen are aware that it is God speaking rather than the prophet.

Our interest in the noun *davar* meaning "speech" or "word" is in its use to mean "the word of God." Appearing this way 394 times in the Old Testament, its usage usually involves commandments, prophecy and words of help to God's people.

The New Testament has the same ring of authority as does the Old. Jesus proclaimed good news, and His hearers said, "No man ever spoke like this man!" (John 7:46). But Jesus also acted, and the events of His life were without parallel. "We never saw anything like this!" wrote one of His contemporaries (Mark 2:12). Yet these same events, unparalleled though they were, were still overshadowed by His death and resurrection.

The authority of the New Testament lies in the person of Jesus Christ—His acts, His words—and in His disciples' proclamation of what God would do for men who enter by faith into a living relationship with the resurrected Christ.

The Bible Has Unity

The Bible is made up of 66 separate "books" and was written and edited over a period of approximately 1400 years. What unifies these 66 separate books? What makes them hang together? Or do they? What unifies the vast quantity of materials in the Bible? There are certain basic themes that unify the books of the Bible.

The Old and New Testaments emphasize the action of God as Creator. There are many facets to the subject of creation, but the Bible stresses one fact: God has brought into existence all that is. He makes what He wants for the purposes He has in mind.

Creation involves both the physical universe and all living things, but it also involves God's action in transforming a rebel into a disciple. This is part of God's current creative action.

Creation also has a future dimension. This future aspect gives meaning and unity to the Bible and history (see Isa. 65:17; 2 Pet. 3:13; Rev. 21, 22). History begins

29

with creation and will end with creation when the final removal of sin and rebellion will climax the "new creation."

The action of God with His people, Israel, draws together all the details of their lives. The theme of promise and fulfillment runs through Israel's history from the time that God spoke to Abraham and told him He would make of him a new nation (Gen. 12:2) until the birth of Jesus, the Messiah of Israel. God renewed His promises, gave new promises, clarified earlier promises and fulfilled some promises. The evidence of promise and fulfillment for Israel and then for the rest of mankind has continued since the Incarnation.

The choice of Israel as a nation, the covenant with Israel, and the role of Israel among the nations are the unfolding of promise and fulfillment. Though there is diversity in the total life of a people, there is unity in the unfolding of God's plan for those who are His own.

The action of God in Christ unites the Bible. Christ's acts had more meaning than was unfolded during His life on earth, for He Himself unifies history and the Scriptures.

Christ gave meaning to all of God's action in the past, so that Paul could write: "But when the time had fully come, God sent forth his Son, born of woman, born under the law, to redeem those who were under the law, so that we might receive adoption as sons" (Gal. 4:4,5).

Christ also gave meaning to all that God would do in the future. He fulfilled the Old Testament promises and came to make disciples of all nations. He made the concept of "the people of God" far broader than the Old Testament Jews understood, and so it is in the New Testament that the idea emerges of the solidarity of the people of God in Christ.

Yet the actual unfolding of this new concept comes

through history itself. "There is no Jew or Greek, there is no slave or free, there is no male or female because you are all one in Christ Jesus" (Gal. 3:28, authors' translation). This is Paul's pronouncement to the early Church, and it was a revolutionary idea.

We all know that sexual distinctions and particular responsibilities of husbands and wives are still here. Though distinctions between Jew and Gentile are said in the New Testament to be ended, anti-Semitism lives on. Slavery still exists in various forms. But these facts do not annul the unifying force of God's action in Christ. The Christian church is—or ought to be—a present sample of what will be when God's kingdom comes, when His will is done on earth as it is in heaven (see Matt. 6:10).

God's creative acts among those who are believers in Christ form a potent unifying factor. In the Old Testament, people are divided into two groups—Jews and Gentiles. But in the New Testament, a third group is created by God. Both Jews and Gentiles who are joined to Christ by faith are created "into one new man" (Eph. 2:15). This third group is God's way of making peace between Jew and Gentile because both are transformed in Christ into something new and distinct—the Church.

Much of the New Testament consists of letters written to individual churches, to groups of Christians over a wide geographical area or to individual believers. The New Testament concept of the unity of all believers in Christ binds these diverse groups together. The New Testament is a unity not only because Christ's words and deeds are central to it, but because the local groups of believers who proclaimed the good news are bound together in a living tie with the risen Lord.

As Christians, they have distinct characteristics involving their whole outlook on life. They show a pur-

31

pose and power different from that of non-Christians. All of this points to the creative activity of God.

The Bible Has Variety

The Bible is unique not only because of its unifying factors, but also because it has such great variety. Just as the unity of the Bible lies in the relationships it reveals between God and His people and the convictions of those within these relationships, so the diversity of the Bible also lies in relationships.

God not only controls these great differences, but also uses them to clarify the meaning of life and His relationships to man. In the Bible, man is viewed realistically rather than poetically.

God's actions vary in His dealings with His people. He takes into account all factors as He works out His own counsel in history. God's dealings with the apostle Paul are a typical example. Paul was imprisoned at various times in Jerusalem, Caesarea and Rome. And as each of his prison experiences was different, so was God's action toward Paul in these prison situations. Consequently, Paul accomplished as much for the advance of the gospel in prison as outside of prison.

God's people responded in various ways to God's leading. We know little from the Bible about those who lived before the time of Abraham. But from Abraham to the close of the New Testament period, the people of God lived in Palestine, Egypt, Assyria, Babylonia and around the whole of the Mediterranean.

Sometimes the nation Israel governed itself, as in the days of the Judges and during the reign of Saul, David and Solomon. But after that period, Israel was often oppressed by foreign powers. The situation of the people swung from one end of the pendulum to the other, and so did their responses.

During the reign of Josiah (640 to 609 B.C.) the nation prospered, worshiped God, and brought Him their thanksgiving. The Israelites were also prosperous under Solomon, but during the latter part of his reign the people began to turn away from God.

Sometimes God's judgment brought them to repentance, as in the time of Nehemiah (Neh. 8); other times, as in the times of Jeremiah and Amos, the people responded to their prophets with resentment.

The varying needs of those to whom the message comes also make for differences in the way it is presented. For this reason, a holy life and consecrated living are presented in various ways to the seven churches in Revelation (Rev. 2, 3).

God spoke to His people through different types of messengers. The words and acts recorded in the Bible show the distinct personality traits and thought patterns of each of the prophets and apostles. This diversity in the style and characteristics of the various biblical writers has occupied scholars in painstaking analysis for over a hundred years.

For example, the story of the woman who was healed from a flow of blood after hemorrhaging for 12 years is narrated in three of the Gospels: Matthew 9:20; Mark 5:25 and Luke 8:43. Mark briskly tells of the woman's trying experience at the hands of many physicians for many years. She has only grown worse (Mark 5:26).

Luke does not mention any of the woman's adverse experiences. He says simply that she was a difficult case who "could not be healed by any one" (Luke 8:43). Matthew gives neither of these descriptions of her illness. These differences in the record show the background of the writers and their different interests.

Mark wanted to show why the woman was so insistent—she was progressively deteriorating. Luke, as a physician, simply said she was a very difficult case and that no one could heal her. Yet all three Gospels agree on the central elements: a woman with a long-standing illness, her touching Christ's garment and her faith being the reason for her cure. These differences in detail help the Bible convey rich, warm, human experiences.

The purposes of the writers also bring differences. This is seen in the contrasts between the historical accounts in Kings and Chronicles. Chronicles tells only the history of the southern kingdom—the tribes of Judah and Benjamin, while Kings tells about both northern and southern kingdoms.

God's messengers had various perspectives. What of the wide differences which confront us when we seriously examine biblical teachings on such doctrines as election, the second coming of Christ or sanctification? Through the centuries, Christians have differed as to how various passages on the same subject should be integrated and which passage should receive the most emphasis.

Remember that each biblical writer or speaker has perspective intentionally limited by God. Paul makes this clear when he writes: "For our knowledge is imperfect and our prophecy is imperfect; but when the perfect comes, the imperfect will pass away. . . . Now I know in part; then I shall understand fully, even as I have been fully understood" (1 Cor. 13:9–12).

It is clear that none of God's inspired servants received *all* the truth. Each was given certain fragments. Even if we could integrate perfectly all that has been revealed—a task of no mean proportions—the result would still be fragmentary.

Someday our limited perspective will be replaced by full understanding. But since God Himself is the unifying force in the midst of diversity, we know that the diversity plays just as great a role in God's purpose as does the unity. This, too, contributes to the uniqueness of the Bible.

The Bible Claims Inspiration

Any discussion of inspiration of the Bible must reckon with two important factors: First, what do the writers of the Scriptures say about the Bible's inspiration? Second, how do their writings help us to understand the nature of inspiration as well as the fact of inspiration?

The biblical writers say that God's action brought the Scriptures into being. "All scripture is inspired by God" (2 Tim. 3:16; see 3:14–17). "First of all you must understand this, that no prophecy of scripture is a matter of one's own interpretation, because no prophecy ever came by the impulse of man, but men moved by the Holy Spirit spoke from God" (2 Pet. 1:20,21). This is a picture of men who spoke and wrote with a God-directed sense of urgency so that they spoke and wrote as divinely energized persons.

When we speak of "verbal inspiration" we are talking about language inspiration, involving a meaningful association of words that are kept in the author's thought pattern. Perhaps Paul had this in mind when he wrote to the Corinthians, "And we impart this in words not taught by human wisdom but taught by the Spirit" (1 Cor. 2:13).

Paul was also aware that God-inspired messages were sometimes regarded by some listeners and readers as merely human utterances. That is why he thanks God that the Thessalonians did not take his oral message to be merely the words of a traveling Jewish teacher, "And we also thank God constantly for this, that when you received the word of God which you heard from us, you accepted it not as the word of men but as what it really

is, the word of God, which is at work in you believers"
(1 Thess. 2:13).

*The Scriptures themselves clearly claim to be inspired
of God.* How about the nature of inspiration? What effect did the divine energizing of God's Spirit actually
have on the words of the writers?

Did they sit down and write what the Spirit of God
whispered in their ears, much as a secretary writes what
her employer dictates? Apparently not, for the writers
exhibit great differences in style.

Did inspiration mean that all material came direct
from God and apart from any human sources? Not at all.
It is true that God often revealed Himself and truths
about Himself to His servants in dreams, visions and
other means. And it seems apparent that God supplies
to His inspired servants interpretations of significant
events, such as the exodus of the Jews from Egypt and
also the death and resurrection of Christ. But the writers
of Scripture also used materials from their own times
and culture.

The writers apparently used source materials available to them in documents and information handed
down by word of mouth. For example, Luke prefaces his
Gospel with the words, "Inasmuch as many have undertaken to compile a narrative of the things which have
been accomplished among us, just as they were delivered to us by those who from the beginning were
eyewitnesses and ministers of the word, it seemed good
to me also, having followed all things closely for some
time past, to write an orderly account for you, most
excellent Theophilus, that you may know the truth concerning the things of which you have been informed"
(Luke 1:1–4). Luke here clearly states that he used
material given by eyewitnesses of the life of Christ.

In the Old Testament books of Kings and Chronicles,

the writers often refer to other longer accounts of the lives of the kings. In 2 Kings 15, there are seven references to longer accounts in the "Book of the Chronicles of the Kings of Israel" (2 Kings 15:6,11,15,21,26,31,36). This reference is *not* to the 1 and 2 Chronicles in the Bible but to books not available to us today.

In 2 Chronicles 12:15 (and in several other places) there are references to the "chronicles of Shemaiah the prophet and of Iddo the seer." First Kings 11:41 refers to "the book of the acts of Solomon."

The biblical writers did not always write with the precise accuracy demanded by scholarly writings of our day. They used approximations, general identifications and popular descriptions familiar to their own times.

When we examine the main purpose of the writers and see how careful and devoted they were to their purpose, their lack of preoccupation with minor details becomes an asset rather than a liability.

The frequent differences in the Gospels give vitality and freshness to the accounts. If four people witness an automobile accident, they will all say something different about it. The accounts will not be identical except in major details. The same is true of the Gospel accounts of the life of Christ, especially regarding Passion Week, which all four writers record in some detail. The differences indicate that the information came from eyewitnesses and that there was no effort by the early Church to polish and harmonize the accounts as some have imagined. There is basic agreement without artificiality and common convictions without a monotonous pattern of details.

In the light of what biblical writers claim and what they do, it seems clear that inspiration involves God acting in the lives and words of His chosen servants in such a way that the Scriptures they wrote convey to men what God wants men to know. In the Scriptures we have all that God chose to preserve so that we can know the infallible truths He conveyed to men of earlier generations.

The Bible Tells Us About God

God did not give us the Bible to tickle our imaginations or to give us grounds for profound theological debates. He gave us His Word—His revealing of Himself—so that we could know Him. That revelation culminated in the coming of Jesus Christ, the incarnate God. The Bible reveals God and His relationship with men so that we, too, can have a living relationship with the living God.

To some extent, the Bible can be considered a "case study book" of man and his relationship to God. It recounts the experiences of many people who loved and served God, and many who refused to acknowledge God and who "walked in wickedness." We see men and women at their best and men and women at their worst. The Bible includes history, poetry, prophecy, exhortation, parables, visions—all there to help us know God and serve Him.

It is a book worth our most careful study so that we can learn from it what God intended for us to learn about Himself, ourselves, and the world in which we live. It is the most important book ever written and it demands our closest attention and careful study if we are to see what God is actually saying to us. That is what sound biblical interpretation is all about.

The Bible is our guidebook in knowing God, in pointing the way to a vital, living fellowship with the Holy One who is creator and Lord. "The unfolding of thy words gives light. . . . the sum of thy word is truth" (Ps. 119:130,160).

WHY ARE THERE SO MANY TRANSLATIONS? 4

Words and ideas usually lose something when translated from one language to another. A good translator must be the master of both the original language and the language into which he is translating. Most of us must struggle to find the right words even in our native language to express the feeling, idea, or fact we want to communicate.

The ways we put certain phrases together and our verbal or written inflections often reveal more than the actual words we use. The translator must try to capture all of these nuances, rephrase them into another language and still communicate those important shades of meaning! Because this is so difficult, the translation often comes out with the nuances of the translator rather than those of the original writer or speaker. Each new translation endeavors to convey more accurately what the writers meant to say.

The Bible Was Written in Three Languages

Each of the three languages in which the Bible was

written—Aramaic, Hebrew, and koine Greek—involves specific problems.

Parts of Daniel and Nehemiah were written in Aramaic. The Aramaic language has been dead for many centuries. Translators must depend on ancient secular manuscripts (such as the Elephantine papyri, consisting of letters, contracts, community happenings, etc.) to reveal the grammar and vocabulary of Aramaic.

Hebrew, in which most of the Old Testament was written, died as a spoken language about 350 B.C. It has, however, been revived in modern Israel. Although modern Hebrew was taken from ancient Hebrew it has already changed considerably, because so many new words have had to be added in keeping with modern times and culture. This is not surprising, for language is always dynamic—constantly changing and developing. Even the Hebrew of the early parts of the Old Testament is not the same as that written 500 years later.

The New Testament was written in koine Greek, which represents a certain period in the development of the Greek language. Like many other languages, modern Greek has flattened out—become simpler, with fewer cases of nouns, fewer moods of verbs, etc. New Testament Greek is quite different from modern Greek.

Mastery of biblical languages requires a lifetime of study. Many fine scholars have given their lives to such study and every student of the Bible has profited from their work.

Most Christians know little about biblical languages nor will they ever become masters of them. But all of us can become aware of the problems involved in language and the limitations these place upon us. We will then be less likely to make the kinds of errors in interpreting the Bible that easily arise from attaching undue emphasis to questionable words.

Biblical Language More Oral than Written

All of the Bible was written many centuries before the invention of the printing press. The biblical languages (Hebrew, Aramaic and Greek) were used far more in speaking than in writing. To early people, the spoken word was much more important than it is to us. Most people could not read or write, so nearly all their communications were in speech.

When the ancient Hebrew and Aramaic languages were written, they were written without vowels. For this reason, the actual sounds and pronunciations of Hebrew and Aramaic words are surrounded by some mystery. Only the consonants were written and the exact word had to be determined by the context.

It is not always easy to determine the vowels by context. If this principle were applied to the English language, the words farm, firm, from, frame, form and forum would all be written "frm." Often it could be difficult to determine the correct word from the context. A sentence reading "He chose the frm" might mean he chose the farm or the frame, or the forum, or the firm.

Between A.D. 500 and 600—centuries *after* Hebrew had died as a spoken language—a group of men known as the Massoretic scholars decided that something should be done to preserve the pronunciation of the Hebrew words. The Hebrew text had been handed down through the centuries by hand copying and it was written with only the consonant sounds. The Massoretic scholars now added "vowel points" to the Hebrew words. By placing a point or a dot at a certain position above or below or within the consonant letters, the scholars indicated which vowels they thought belonged in the words. This has become known as the Massoretic text, and while it is helpful, it is by no means indisputable. After all, the Massoretic scholars had no way of knowing for sure whether a combination of letters like "frm" meant farm, forum, or firm, if the context did not make it clear. In the Old Testament, there are a number of passages where the original meaning is not sure.

For example, in Hebrews 11:21, the New Testament writer spoke of Jacob's death this way: "By faith Jacob, when dying, blessed each of the sons of Joseph, bowing in worship over the head of his *staff*" (italics added).

But our Genesis account of this story in 47:31 reads: "Then Israel bowed himself upon the head of his *bed*" (italics added).

Why the difference? The Hebrew text has the equivalent of the letters MTTH. The translators of the Old Testament version used by the writer of Hebrews thought the vowels should be added to form the word *matteh*, which means staff or rod. Those who prepared the later Massoretic text and other more recent Hebrew scholars believed the vowels should be those in the word *mittah*, which means couch or bed. So our Genesis account in English reads "bed" but the Hebrews account reads "staff."

Hebrew and Greek Were Rich Languages

Hebrew was a rich language—Greek even more so. Not only was the vocabulary so extensive that it permitted fine delineations of meaning, but also the grammar and syntax were capable of expressing delicate differences. English cannot do this.

Sometimes the English language does not express all that the biblical languages expressed. This language difference can be just enough to convey erroneous ideas. For example, in English we cannot differentiate between *you* singular and *you* plural. In our highly individualistic society, we tend to read every you as meaning an individual. But often in the Scriptures, written in a culture that stressed corporate solidarity and group consciousness, the *you* is plural.

Philippians 1:6 reads, "I am sure that he who began a good work in you will bring it to completion at the day of Jesus Christ." We usually read this verse as an individual promise that "he who began a good work in *me*." But the Greek text shows that the *you* in this case is plural. It refers to a group—the church at Philippi. Now the meaning changes from a promise to the individual to a promise that his church will prevail. "He who began a good work among you [plural] will keep on working until its completion in the day of Jesus Christ."

How can we know whether *you* is singular or plural? One way is to consult a good commentary. (See the bibliography for a list of helpful commentaries.)

Sometimes differences can be found by consulting other versions where the translator may have rearranged the sentence to make clear whether the word is singular or plural.

Sometimes a careful study of the context would show what is meant. Actually, this is true of Phillippians 1:6, but we often do not study whole passages as we should.

The verbs in the biblical languages give greater depth of meaning than do our English verbs. For example, in the Greek there is an aorist tense that expresses totality or wholeness of action. Greek also has perfect tenses which describe the action as a *state* (in the past, present, or future). Greek has present and imperfect tenses that describe action as *continuous*.

Although English has compound tenses (i.e., he is believing, he has believed) they are not used as freely as their Greek equivalents, and translators must often surrender the fine distinctions in the effort to make a translation highly readable and in keeping with our idiomatic language. For example, a literal translation of 1 Corinthians 1:18 would read, "For the word of the cross is to those who are in the process of perishing, foolishness; but to us who are in the process of being saved, the power of God."

The verb in the Greek is the present participle. This becomes awkward and difficult to convey in English. The *King James* translators said, "For the preaching of the cross is to them that perish, foolishness; but unto us which are saved, it is the power of God."

The *Revised Standard Version* did better by saying, "who are perishing" and "who are being saved," but even then the full force of the *process* idea does not come through in English.

The biblical languages are usually more precise than English. The layman will not master enough Greek or Hebrew or Aramaic to make use of these fine lines of precision, but we can realize our limitations because of this and refrain from pronouncements based on a pronoun or past tense or an English grammatical construction that may be unable to express the full force of the original language.

On the other hand, there are some instances in which *Greek is less precise than English.* And this introduces other problems.

The current discussions about biblical teachings on the role of women in the church are complicated by the fact that the Greek language uses the same word *gune* for "women" as for "wife" and the word *aner* means both man and husband.

In 1 Timothy 2:12, the *RSV* reads "I permit no woman to teach or to have authority over men; she is to keep silent." This verse could also be translated, "I permit no wife to teach or have authority over her husband."

In 1 Timothy 3:8–13, there is a discussion about quali-

44

fications for deacons. In the middle of the paragraph, verse 11 states, "The women likewise must be serious, no slanderers, but temperate, faithful in all things" (*RSV*).

The *King James* translated it "Even so must their wives be...."

The word *gune* does not tell us whether it means wives, women in general, or women deacons. The only guide to meaning in this case must be the context, and the differences between translations indicate that even biblical scholars do not agree as to what the original writer had in mind.

Original writings of the Bible and early copies of them were written in ancient style. This meant there were no spaces between words, no punctuation, no paragraphs, no capitals and small letters. Everything was in the equivalent of capital letters.

Imagine a line from Romans 3:27,28 the way it appeared in early manuscripts. It would have been in Greek, of course, but the English equivalent might be something like this: THENWHATBECOMESOFOURBOAST INGITISEXCLUDEDONWHATPRINCIPLEONTHEPRINCIPLE OFWORKSNOBUTONTHEPRINCIPLEOFFAITHFORWEHOLD THATAMANISJUSTIFIEDBYFAITHAPARTFROMTHELAW.

The translator must decide where sentences begin and end, where to place paragraphs, how it should be punctuated, what should be in quotation marks.

The decisions were not always easy. In John 3:15,16, there has been a difference of opinion as to whether the famous John 3:16 was part of the words of Christ to Nicodemus, or whether they are the words of the Apostle John. Some versions place the end of the quotation after verse 15, while others place the quotation mark at the end of verse 21.

Division by chapters and verses was not added until

45

the Middle Ages. These divisions make it much easier for us to find our way around in the Scriptures, but they may also make us think that the writer arranged his thoughts in the same groupings that appear in our Bibles. The translators' divisions are usually right, but they can be wrong.

New Testament Quoted the Old Differently

Other confusing situations stem from the language problems. A serious Bible student soon discovers that a New Testament writer often quotes verses from the Old Testament. If the student looks up the Old Testament reference (usually indicated in a marginal note) he may find that the Old Testament text does not read the same way it is quoted in the New Testament.

For example, Hebrews 12:6 quotes from Proverbs 3:12. The Hebrews passage quotes the Old Testament as saying, "For the Lord disciplines him whom he loves, and chastises every son whom he receives." But Proverbs 3:12 in the Old Testament actually says, "For the Lord reproves him whom he loves, as a father the son in whom he delights." Why the difference?

This quotation, like a majority of the quotations in the New Testament, is from the Septuagint. The Septuagint is the Greek translation of the Old Testament that was made between 250 and 150 B.C. During this period of Greek conquest, many of the Jews left Palestine and settled in countries around the Mediterranean and began to speak the Greek language. Their children needed the Old Testament in the Greek language they now spoke. The early Church grew mostly among these Greek-speaking Jews and among Greek-speaking Gentiles. Thus the Septuagint became the "Bible" of the early Church.

The writer of Hebrews used the Septuagint when he

quoted Proverbs 3:12 in his letter. The translators of the Septuagint thought that the Hebrew consonants in the last part of the verse made the most sense when they had the vowel sounds that made it mean "and he causes pain." Modern translators believed the verse made better sense with the vowels that mean "as a Father."

The writer of the Epistle to the Hebrews quotes exclusively from the Septuagint, probably indicating that he did not know the Hebrew version. Even Paul often used the Septuagint. In fact, 51 of the 93 Old Testament quotations that he uses are from the Septuagint, even though he also knew the Hebrew text. He realized that most of his readers knew Greek but not Hebrew. Quotations from the Septuagint account for many of the differences between our Old Testament readings and the way passages are quoted in the New Testament.

Jesus spoke and taught in Aramaic. The New Testament Gospels recording the life and words of Jesus were written in Greek. However, the common language of the people in Palestine among whom Jesus lived was not Greek but Aramaic—a sort of first cousin to Hebrew. Many of the people of Jesus' day were bilingual, speaking both Aramaic and Greek; Greek was the language of commerce. Jesus was undoubtedly bilingual, but He spoke Aramaic as He walked along the roads and taught the people who gathered around Him. Aramaic was their "language of the heart"—that which they used around their own tables and which spoke to them the most intimately and deeply.

The words of Jesus as they were originally recorded in Greek by Matthew, Mark, Luke, and John were *translations of what Jesus actually said in Aramaic.* The sayings of Jesus no doubt circulated orally, both in Aramaic and in Greek. This probably accounts for some of the differences among the Gospel accounts, for trans-

47

lations by nature allow for more than one possible way of expressing an idea.

The nature of languages and the problems involved in handing down writings over a period of thousands of years and translated from one language to another are highly complex.

Today's Christian must base his beliefs on the *total* message of the Bible, not on individual verses or phrases chosen because they please him.

WHAT IS
THE BIBLE
TALKING
ABOUT? 5

How do you feel when someone takes something you have said or written and lifts it out of the context in which you used it so that its meaning is distorted? You probably are frustrated and angry because you cannot deny that you said or wrote these words, but the meaning now given to them is not what you originally intended.

How frustrated the biblical writers probably would be if they could hear how the things they wrote are often used! Preachers and laymen alike are guilty of this. Remarkably fine sermons have often been hung on a line or two of Scripture taken out of context. Regardless of how fine and uplifting the sermon may be, it is a kind of dishonesty to try to give added authority to our ideas by implying that the Scriptures we are quoting uphold what we are saying.

Determine the Context of the Passage
The exact meaning of a passage of Scripture is usually

controlled by what precedes and what follows a specific thought. This is referred to as the "context" of the passage. Biblical writers usually expressed themselves in series of related ideas, sometimes tied together loosely by a general theme, but generally supported by the ideas preceding and following the specific thought.

The first thing we should do is read through the whole book. Suppose, for example, we are studying Ephesians 3:4–6. What is the general purpose of the letter to the Ephesians? We cannot know this until we read the whole of Ephesians. By reading through the entire book we can see the total thrust of the message. As we read we should summarize in a few words the main point of each paragraph. These notes could be written in the margin of a wide-margin Bible, or on a separate sheet of paper. Although a summary prepared by a biblical scholar may be more correct professionally than yours, it will never stay with you as firmly as your own summary will.

Make your own headings. Even though many Bibles include paragraph headings, you will learn more if you make your own. If you went through the book of Ephesians assigning paragraph headings, you would find that most of the first chapter is a picture of God's glorious plan of salvation and a prayer that the readers may know and experience that glory.

Chapters 2 and 3 discuss the unity of all believers in Christ. Ephesians 2:1–10 tells what it means to be made alive in Christ. Ephesians 2:11–22 discusses the Gentiles' equal share with Jewish Christians in the blessings of the new life in Christ.

Chapter 3 deals with this remarkable union of Gentile and Jewish believers in Christ.

Chapters 4–6 give practical instructions on how the believer is to conduct himself in the light of his position in Christ.

Check what comes before the particular passage you are studying. After considering the overall content of the book, look at the immediate context. Ephesians 3:4–6 is part of a section where Paul discusses the relationship of Jew and Gentile to God. Immediately preceding it (2:14–16), Paul develops the idea of the union of Jews and Gentiles in the Church. God, through the reconciliation of Christ, makes the two—Jew and Gentile—into one person, the Christian. All Christians (Jews and Gentiles) are a part of one body—the Church. Through Christ, Jews and Gentiles may approach God in one Spirit (2:18). The Gentiles who were once "strangers and sojourners" are now fellow citizens with the saints—the Jewish saints—and all are now part of the "household of God" (2:19).

Knowing what is in chapter 2 is essential to understanding Ephesians 3:4–6: "When you read this you can perceive my insight into the mystery of Christ, which was not made known to the sons of men in other generations as it has now been revealed to his holy apostles and prophets by the Spirit; that is, how the Gentiles are fellow heirs, members of the same body, and partakers of the promise in Christ Jesus through the gospel."

Ephesians 3:6 reads, "how the Gentiles are fellow heirs, members of the same body, and partakers of the promise in Christ Jesus through the gospel." If we did not know what came before this in chapter 2, we would ask, "Fellow heirs with whom? Members of the same body as who? Partakers with whom of the promise in Christ Jesus?" But the previous chapter has already told us that Paul is talking about the "mystery" of Jewish believers and Gentile believers being brought together in Christ.

It is also important to examine what follows your particular passage. Look at Ephesians 3:7–10: "Of this

51

gospel I was made a minister according to the gift of God's grace which was given me by the working of his power. To me, though I am the very least of all the saints, this grace was given, to preach to the Gentiles the unsearchable riches of Christ, and to make all men see what is the plan of the mystery hidden for ages in God who created all the things; that through the church the manifold wisdom of God might now be made known to the principalities and powers in the heavenly places."

Here Paul explains that his main activity was to bring this good news to the Gentiles. To them he proclaimed what had previously been a secret (v. 9). This "mystery" or secret was the way that God would bring all people, Jews and Gentiles, into a living relationship with Himself.

Study Parallel Writings in the Bible

The same ideas or teachings are often found in several parts of the Bible. One passage reinforces or throws additional light on another. These are called parallel passages. In a true parallel, one writer often gives a fuller version of an incident or parable or teaching than other writers. Consulting the various accounts gives a more complete picture. However, while parallels are extremely helpful they can also be dangerous.

Sometimes what seems parallel is not. This is true where one passage seems to be restating an idea found elsewhere in the Bible so the reader tends to give the same meaning to both ideas. But it may not be a true parallel. Only the context will tell whether or not the ideas are parallel.

For example, in Ephesians 3:3–6, the "mystery of Christ" is the Jew and Gentile being made "one new person" by belief in Christ. But Paul uses the word "mystery" again in Colossians 1:25–27: "I became a minister according to the divine office which was given to me for you, to make the word of God fully known, the mystery hidden for ages and generations but now made manifest to his saints. To them God chose to make known how great among the Gentiles are the riches of the glory of this mystery, which is Christ in you, the hope of glory."

This sounds somewhat like the passage in Ephesians. But here Paul clearly defines the "mystery" as "Christ in you, the hope of glory." The two ideas are certainly related, but they are not identical. Ephesians 3:6 cannot be used to define the mystery in Colossians 1:27 or vice versa. The Ephesians verses discuss and define a *part* of the mystery which is discussed in Colossians—Christ in you, the hope of glory.

A good example of true parallel writings is the four Gospels. Four different writers recorded the teachings and life of Christ. A parallel study of their accounts has particular significance. Sometimes Jesus' teachings are arranged chronologically; other times they are grouped by subject matter. No doubt Jesus often repeated Himself in His travels throughout Galilee and Perea. Sometimes He expounded to His disciples more at length on a particular subject than He did to the crowds who gathered to hear Him.

To understand Jesus' teachings on any subject, we must gather together all of these parallels, carefully considering them in their context.

For example, Matthew 5:31,32 gives a brief statement regarding the teaching of Jesus on divorce. However, in Matthew 19:3–12 and in Mark 10:2–12 there are fuller statements that give more background and setting for this teaching of Jesus.

Twice Matthew records teachings about "cutting off your hand if it causes you to sin," but the passage in

Matthew 18:8,9 gives more context than the one in Matthew 5:29,30.

Words do not always have the same meaning. In dealing with parallel passages, we tend to assume that the same words have to have the same meaning. Yet we know this is not true in our own language. Consider the word "rest." If a man in the middle of a hot afternoon says he wants to rest, he probably means he wants a nap. If a doctor says the man needs a rest, he may mean he ought to take a trip to relieve the tension of his job. If we say "he was laid to rest in a quiet garden" we mean he was buried. In each case, rest has a different meaning.

As a biblical example Paul uses the word "flesh" in several ways. In Romans 8:12,13 he says, "So then, brethren, we are debtors, not to the flesh, to live according to the flesh—for if you live according to the flesh you will die, but if by the Spirit you put to death the deeds of the body you will live." This is part of a long passage in which Paul contrasts "flesh" with "Spirit."

Paul uses "flesh" with a different meaning in Philippians 1:22–24: "If it is to be life in the flesh, that means fruitful labor for me. Yet which I shall choose I cannot tell. I am hard pressed between the two. My desire is to depart and be gone with Christ, for that is far better. But to remain in the flesh is more necessary on your account." In this passage, "flesh" obviously refers to man as a finite creature.

The context must determine the meaning of a biblical word, just as context determines meaning in our own speech.

Recognize Topical Groupings
Some selections of the Old and New Testaments record no context. Proverbs and Ecclesiastes are collections of sayings, proverbs, and epigrams for which no

immediate context is given. However, the editor or collector of these sayings often grouped them together topically.

This kind of grouping also occurs sometimes in the Gospels, especially in the sayings of Jesus. For example, in Luke 16:14–18 five topics are discussed in five verses.

verse	*topic*
14. The Pharisees, who were lovers of money, heard all this, and they scoffed at him.	The Pharisees ridiculed Jesus for His teaching on wealth.
15. But he said to them, "You are those who justify yourselves before men, but God knows your hearts; for what is exalted among men is an abomination in the sight of God.	Jesus declares God's knowledge of men's hearts.
16. "The law and the prophets were until John; since then the good news of the Kingdom of God is preached, and every one enters it violently.	The law and the prophets were until John, plus the proclamation and response to the Kingdom of God.
17. "But it is easier for heaven and earth to pass away, than for one dot of the law to become void.	The disappearance of heaven and earth are easier than the invalidity of the smallest part of the Law.

18. "Everyone who di-   Divorce
    vorces his wife and
    marries another
    commits adultery,
    and he who marries
    a woman divorced
    from her husband
    commits adultery."

What can you do in these situations? One method is to try to find genuine parallels in another book by the same author or in another book from the same general time period. For example, in Luke 16:18 regarding divorce, there is a fuller account with more context in Matthew 19:3–12.

Faithful examination of context will help us appreciate the genuine authority of the Bible.

Determining the Context

1. Note carefully the immediate context—what precedes and what follows the passage to get the general train of thought.

2. Study any parallel passages in the same book.

3. Observe carefully any parallel teachings in another book by the same author or in other books by different authors. Be sure to analyze the purpose and thought development so you can determine whether the author is actually discussing the same idea.

4. The shorter the passage (such as a single verse or part of a verse) the greater is the danger in ignoring context. "A text without its context is only a pretext."

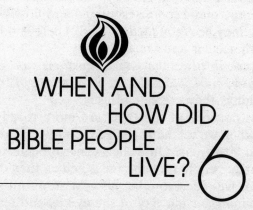

WHEN AND HOW DID BIBLE PEOPLE LIVE? 6

No event occurs in a vacuum. Every person lives within a historical and cultural situation and is influenced by it. Every biblical event and teaching arose from and is a part of a particular history and culture.

In one sense, history is what actually happened in a certain period of time. However, *the history we know is actually the historian's selection of factors in the life of an individual, group, nation, or group of nations to give meaning to the acts and purposes of the person, group or nation.* All history, written or oral, is an interpretation of events by the historian, regardless of how objective and honest the historian is trying to be. It cannot be otherwise.

History, as it is conceived by historians, is people-centered. It is the story of persons trying to get along with and by themselves. But the Christian believes that history is more than this—it is the unfolding of God's plan or purpose. The Christian cannot center history exclusively on people and ignore God.

The Bible involves a great deal of history. But in the Scriptures, the actions of people and the actions of God are recorded together. In this kind of history, people meet God in a God-ordained sequence of experiences in which they may become estranged and hostile to God, or they may be reconciled to God. There is no division between secular and sacred history.

Culture involves the habits, customs, tools, institutions, arts, music, and literary productions of any people —all things they create and use.

Most portions of the Bible are more readily understood when we set them against their own historical and cultural situations. Only then can we begin to understand why people thought and acted as they did. Only then are we ready to take the next step to understand the meaning for our day of the events and teachings.

Learn Historical and Cultural Backgrounds

Sometimes historical and cultural backgrounds are difficult to determine. Biblical scholars often disagree as to the date of the writing of certain books. For example, the book of Obadiah has been dated as early as 900 B.C. and as late as 400 B.C. If scholars have a hard time determining when it was written, how can the average Bible student know anything about the historical and cultural background of the book?

Fortunately, the situation is not as hopeless as it might first appear. There *is* general consensus among biblical scholars as to the dates of many of the books of the Bible. Variances as wide as that of Obadiah are the exception rather than the rule.

But even with Obadiah, we are not left dangling, for the historical situation is more important than the precise historical date. The contents of Obadiah show that the historical situation was one of conflict between the descendants of Esau and the descendants of Jacob, his brother. Whether the conflict between the groups occurred in the ninth century or the sixth century or some other century makes little difference in understanding the vision of Obadiah.

On this subject of historical dating it is necessary to admit that biblical scholars often have their own prejudices that tend to control their thinking about the time certain books were written. For example, some scholars are convinced, because of their own theological views, that God never reveals the future to His prophets. Therefore, if God makes disclosures to men, these disclosures must deal only with the past or present. This, of course, makes predictive prophecy impossible. Therefore, *because of his theological views*, such an interpreter will date a book containing prophecy at a time *after* the prophesied event took place. The interpreter may then insist that prophecy is just another way of writing history!

A German phrase, *Sitz im Leben*, has become almost a part of the English language among those who investigate historical backgrounds. It means "life situation," and includes the history and culture of the individual or group or nation being studied.

There is another part of the biblical picture that is equally important, known as *Sitz im Glauben* or "faith situation." It asks, "What is the relationship of this person, or group, or nation to God?" Both the "life situation" and the "faith situation" are important in understanding any passage. But where can we find such information?

Use an Atlas, Dictionary and a Commentary

A good Bible atlas, or dictionary will give much of the geographical, political and cultural information. A good commentary supplies historical information of the "life and faith" situation of the passage being studied. This is often essential if we are to make the right leap from what the passage meant to the first readers to the application of it to our lives today.

For example, a commentary on Paul's letters to the Corinthians should show in nearly every passage the situation of Paul's original readers. The questions the Corinthians wanted Paul to answer came straight from their own "life and faith situations." Christianity had come to Corinth, a city with a long history and distinct cultural patterns. Only when these are understood will the reader understand the significance of Paul's statements on marriage (1 Cor. 7), on conduct in public meetings (1 Cor. 14), on separation from idolatry (2 Cor. 6:14—7:1), and several other subjects.

You should know the geography of the ancient world. Palestine was the crossroads of the Near East. Through this land marched the great leaders of world empires. To the Jews, Palestine was *the land* that God had promised them (Gen. 35:12; Heb. 11:9). The modern Jew, who is often quite irreligious, shares with his ancient Jewish ancestor a passionate devotion to *the land.* In fact, the land has become almost an idol taking the place of God. Many atheistic and agnostic Jews are still ardent Zionists. To the Christian, the land is important as the place where God performed many of His mighty acts.

You should be aware of political settings and backgrounds. Political rulers played an important role in the life of the nation Israel and were an influence on the early Church. Rulers and their attitudes throw light on Scripture passages.

For example, at the time of the birth of Christ, Palestine was ruled by Roman procurators or governors. The Jews hated the Romans and the Romans hated the Jews —both with good reason! Both sides had intermittently tried to irritate each other and to get along together. Antagonisms were running deep at the time of the birth of Christ and it was only a question of when war would begin. In this setting Jesus was born, lived, was put to death, and rose again. In this same atmosphere, the good news of the gospel spread across Palestine, Asia Minor, Greece and Italy. Early Christianity did not have ideal political surroundings.

The serious Bible student also needs to know the political history behind particular incidents. The Samaritan woman with whom Jesus talked at the well of Sychar had behind her 500 years of political conflict with Jews that colored her feelings. Her remarks and the statement, "Now Jews do not associate on friendly terms with Samaritans," in John 4:9 (authors' translation) show that animosity was the accepted way of life—just as animosity is part of the way of life between Jews and Arabs.

You should know as much as can be known about the habits of everyday life. The kind of homes people lived in, their tools, clothing, food, means of travel and other cultural factors sometimes are significant in understanding the Bible.

For example, in the story of Jesus' healing the paralytic man, the accounts say that because of the crowds, four men went up on the roof, opened a hole, and let the sick man down in front of Jesus (see Matt. 9:1–8; Mark 2:1,2; Luke 5:17–26).

If the reader visualizes an American ranch-type home or a two-story bungalow, the idea of tearing up the roof and letting the man down through a hole brings to mind

scenes of destruction and a shower of falling plaster! But
when we understand that a Palestinian home was a simple two- or three-room house with a roof covered by
branches or, in better-class homes, adobe tile, then we
can see how this incident was possible. The four friends
carried the paralytic man up the outside stairs to the
roof. At the place on the roof where they thought they
were directly over Jesus the friends removed some of
the tiles (Luke 5:19), and let the man down through the
opening in front of Jesus.[1] It was a simple matter to then
replace the tile or branches. With the proper background information the story of the paralytic and his
four friends who had faith becomes alive and thrilling.

Another example of how knowing habits of everyday
life can affect the way we understand the Bible can be
seen in Leonardo da Vinci's portrait of the Last Supper.
This moving interpretation of each of the twelve apostles and of Christ has helped to establish in our minds
an erroneous picture that makes the events of that evening hard to understand.

Instead of sitting upright at a long table as in da Vinci's painting, the Jews of that time (like the Greeks)
usually ate in a reclining position. The table for the Last
Supper was probably a U-shaped one, with Jesus in the
center. As the disciples and Jesus reclined on their
couches around the table, Jesus spoke of His betrayal.
John 13:23 records, "One of his disciples, whom Jesus
loved, was lying close to the breast of Jesus." The Gospel then recounts what is obviously a private conversa-
tion between that disciple and Jesus. Knowing the
customs, we can now visualize the Last Supper with the
men lying on couches so that the head of one man would
be close to the breast of the man on his right.

Later that evening, Jesus dipped a morsel into a dish
and gave it to Judas (John 13:26). To us, having one

person dip something into a dish (*KJV* says, "dipped the sop") and hand it to someone else to eat is repulsive. But within Jewish culture it was a symbol of deep friendship. The action of Jesus now becomes moving and significant.

You should know the socio-religious customs of Bible people. In every culture, much of life is determined by socio-religious customs. Birth, marriage, and death are surrounded by socio-religious ceremonies. This was true of the Jews, and the patterns play an important part in understanding the Bible.

After Jesus was born, His parents observed three customary religious ceremonies. They were Jesus' circumcision on the eighth day after His birth when He was named Jesus (Luke 2:21; see also Lev. 12:3), Mary's purification according to the law (Lev. 12:4–7) 33 days later, and at the same time, Jesus' dedication (Luke 2:22–39).

Understanding other customs in Old Testament stories clarifies phrases that may sound strange without knowing the customs. Legal transactions in ancient times often took place at the gate of the city. When we read in the book of Esther that Mordecai is "sitting at the king's gate" (Esther 2:19), we know that he was one of the judges of his day. His office was at the king's gate.

You should know something of the economy of the people in Bible times. Decisions people made were often influenced by their economy. Absence of rainfall meant famine. Earthquakes blotted out whole cities. The relocating of the entire population of a city as a result of the ravages of war affected economic decisions. The conquering country often removed and deported whole social groups to other countries.

For example, many Jews were deported to Babylon when the southern kingdom fell in 586 B.C. When Cyrus, the Persian ruler, invited Jews to go back to their land beginning in 539 B.C., many Jews were not interested in returning to Palestine. They had found a stable economy in their adopted land and they were prospering. They looked at the unstable economy of Palestine and found it uninviting.

These factors are rarely referred to in Scripture. The message supersedes all such detail, and the original readers knew all about it anyway. But for us to understand the message and the response of the people to it, we need to know these economic facts.

How Can I Find God's Message?

The message of God as recorded in the Bible nearly always came into a specific historical and cultural situation. The message was deeply relevant to the people in that situation. But what about us? Is it relevant to us?

It is if we can make the leap from the ancient situation to our own. The basic needs and desires of people have not changed significantly. But the thought patterns and language by which they express these needs has changed drastically.

In the Bible the "reins," as translated in the *King James Version*, or kidneys, were usually considered the center of being. Psalm 16:7 reads "My reins also instruct me in the night seasons" and Revelation 2:23 says, "I am he which searcheth the reins and hearts."

"Bowels" are often referred to as the seat of emotion. In the *King James Version*, Colossians 3:12 says, "Put on therefore, as the elect of God, holy and beloved, bowels of mercies, kindness, humbleness of mind"; 1 John 3:17 says, "But whoso hath this world's good, and seeth his brother have need, and shutteth up his bowels of compassion from him, how dwelleth the love of God in him?" These terms are omitted in the *Revised Stan-*

dard Version where the passage in John reads "yet closes his heart against him."

Sometimes "heart" is used in the Bible as the seat of intellect, "For man believes with his heart and so is justified" (Rom. 10:10). Yet in our culture we do not consider "believing" to be a function of the heart.

In other parts of the world, these ideas must be translated into other forms. In the Sudanic languages of northern Congo, for example, the liver is considered the center of man's inward being. In this culture, Matthew 15:8 should be translated, "These people honor me with their lips, but their liver is far from me." Therefore, the missionary of today must go yet another step and understand the cultural patterns of the people to whom he ministers.

God's message came to man in a distinct cultural setting different from our own. We cannot really understand what it means in our culture unless we first understand what it meant in the original culture.

Dealing with History and Culture

1. Know as much as you can about the people who are involved in the section of the Bible you are studying.

2. Determine what historical period is most likely for the passage. Remember that it is more important to know the historical situation than the precise historical date.

3. In a Bible atlas, or dictionary, check the places that provide the geographical setting.

4. Note the customs, objects of material culture, or socio-religious relationships in the section you are studying.

5. Try to see how the history preceding the time of the original hearers or readers influenced their responses and attitudes.

6. See how the passage or story transcends its immediate surroundings. While the biblical narrative may have much in common with the history and culture of neighboring people, the differences are often significant.

7. Be sensitive to the similarities and differences between our culture and that of the original writer and his readers. Only then can we make proper applications to ourselves.

Footnote

1. Alfred Edersheim assumes that this house was one of the better dwellings of the middle class. It probably had a U-shaped central courtyard with rooms opening into this courtyard on the inner three sides of the U. The courtyard had one open end (at the top of the U). An overhang extending outward from the U-shaped living quarters permitted those living there to go from one room to another around the courtyard without getting out in the sun or rain. Edersheim thinks that the teachers of the Law and the Pharisees may have been sitting in the guest chamber where Jesus was staying. Other people thronged into the courtyard to listen to Jesus. Jesus stood in the doorway to His guest chamber and spoke to the people in the courtyard. The men took the sick man up on the overhanging roof, removed some of the tiles from the overhang and lowered the man down before Jesus. Alfred Edersheim, *The Life and Times of Jesus the Messiah.* Vol. 1 (Grand Rapids: Wm. B. Eerdmans Pub. Co., 1953), pp. 501–503.

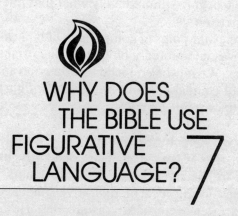

WHY DOES THE BIBLE USE FIGURATIVE LANGUAGE? 7

What is "literal" language and what is "figurative"? In this book, the word "literal" refers to the usual meaning given to words or expressions. "Figurative" means a word or expression represents something else that can be readily compared and understood. When Jesus said, "I am the bread of life" (John 6:35), He used figurative language. He meant that He is to people spiritually what bread is to people physically—the sustainer of life.

Comparisons and imagery are constantly used in explaining things to children. A child asks, "What is a cloud like inside? Is it like cotton?" And a parent answers, "No, a cloud is not like cotton. It is more like thick fog." Something known to the child by experience is used to explain something not known—he has never felt a cloud.

We also use short figures of speech freely in our own language. When we say, "He is an eager beaver," or "She is an iceberg," the meaning is clear to the listener. It does *not* mean that the man has a flat tail like a beaver or that the woman is huge like an iceberg. It refers instead to *one* important characteristic that the person shares in common with whatever is being compared. And we recognize immediately what that relevant point of comparison is.

The relevant point of comparison of biblical figures of speech was undoubtedly obvious to the original listener or reader. We must also recognize the relevant point (or points) of comparison and *not push the figure of speech beyond that point or points.*

Figures of Speech Are Common in the Bible

Jesus, the Master Teacher, constantly used things familiar to His listeners to teach new truths. So skillful was Jesus in His use of figurative language that His listeners often were hardly aware that He had used a figure, but His message came home immediately and sharply.

Jesus chose His figurative language from every area of life familiar to His listeners. He talked of foxes, sheep, birds, the mustard seed, the leafing of trees, fruit growing, the signs of the weather.

He chose imagery from wedding customs, father-son relationships, qualities of children, parts of houses (door, key), household tasks such as mending, sweeping, sewing, cooking.

For Jesus, imagery was the language of life. Old Testament prophets also used imagery profusely. It is important to know how to recognize this imagery.

Jesus often used parables to illustrate a spiritual truth. (This book discusses parables more thoroughly in chapter 11.) Parables are short, fictional stories that present a lesson by comparison. Jesus sometimes taught in parables in order to confuse those who were trying to trick Him into saying something that could be used against Him. Once in a while Jesus had to interpret a parable, but usually the hearers understood its hidden meaning.

In Mark 12:1–12 Jesus told the parable of a man who had a vineyard, rented it out to tenants, and then went to another country. When the vineyard began to bear grapes, he sent servants to the tenants to collect the rental. The tenants beat, stoned, and killed the servants. The owner sent other servants and the tenants treated them the same way. Finally he sent his own son, thinking that the tenants would show more respect for him. But the tenants killed him, too, reasoning that if they killed the heir, the whole vineyard would be theirs. Then Jesus asked, "What will the owner of the vineyard do? He will come and destroy the tenants, and give the vineyard to others." (See also Matt. 21:33–46; Luke 20:9–18.)

All three accounts of this parable include the comment "they perceived that he had told this parable against them" (Matt. 21:45; Luke 20:19; Mark 12:12). The chief priests and the Pharisees recognized immediately what Jesus was saying by the parable—that although the Jews had a unique role as God's chosen instruments to bring men to salvation, they would lose that role by rejecting Christ.

Jesus taught through similes—a comparison explicitly stated with a word such as "like" or "as."

When Jesus sent out the seventy in Luke 10:1–3, He told them exactly what to expect, "Behold, I send you out *as* lambs in the midst of wolves" (italics added). In this figure Jesus indicates that He recognized a growing animosity to Himself. He had fierce enemies (wolves) and the seventy (lambs) had no experience for such conflict. The key word for this simile is "as."

Again, in Matthew 23:37, Jesus looked over Jerusalem and said, "How often would I have gathered your children together *as* a hen gathers her brood under her wings, and you would not!" (italics added). The salient points of comparison are the love, concern and care Jesus wanted to give to His own people, but they chose to follow the familiar road of departure from the God of Israel.

Jesus uses another simile to describe His second coming. Matthew 24:26,27 reads: "So, if they say to you, 'Lo, he is in the wilderness,' do not go out; if they say, 'Lo, he is in the inner rooms,' do not believe it. For as the lightning comes from the east and shines as far as the west, so will be the coming of the Son of man."

The comparison (indicated by "as") is that the coming of Christ will be as visible as the lightning that can be seen from east to west. He apparently used this simile to correct any erroneous ideas of a secret coming of Christ in some desert place or inner room.

Similes are common in the Old and New Testaments. The book of Revelation is profuse with them. Revelation has so many, in fact, that the reader needs to think about each one with these questions: Why did John feel he should use a simile in this place? How does the simile help us to understand the idea being presented? Even with the simile, what is there in this passage that is still unknown to the reader or is understood in only a general way?

While thankful for whatever illumination similes bring, we must not be overzealous in making them say more than they were meant to convey. Similes are like wild flowers: if we cultivate them too generously, they lose their beauty.

Scripture frequently uses metaphors. A metaphor is a figure of speech in which the writer describes one thing in terms of something else. Metaphors are common in both Old and New Testaments.

In Luke 12:32, Jesus said, "Fear not, *little flock*, for it is your Father's good pleasure to give you the kingdom" (italics added).

This same metaphor continues on in John 10:16: "And I have other sheep, that are not of this fold; I must bring them also, and they will heed my voice. So there shall be *one flock*, one shepherd" (italics added). Through this metaphor, Jesus taught His concept of the Church.

Through still another metaphor, Jesus taught that spiritual ties are stronger and more important than physical ties, "My mother and my brothers are those who hear the word of God and do it" (Luke 8:21).

Many metaphors in the Old and New Testaments describe God's power in terms of body parts and physical movements. "Behold, the Lord's hand is not shortened, that it cannot save, or his ear dull, that it cannot hear" (Isa. 59:1). These are technically known as *anthropomorphisms*. Probably the most common is the phrase "the arm of the Lord." We know that God does not have a physical arm nor an ear. Yet this metaphorical language gives a more vivid picture of the power of God than would a theological treatise on the omnipotence of God.

Another kind of metaphor, known as *anthropopathism*, is used to ascribe to God human emotions, feelings and responses. God's *grief* is mentioned in Genesis 6:6 and Ephesians 4:30. God's *wrath* is referred to in John 3:36; Revelation 14:10; 15:1,7 and other places. His *anger* plays a prominent role in Job 9:13; Jonah 3:9 and Mark 3:5.

Is this metaphorical language? Does not God actually experience grief, wrath, and anger? The answer is yes, but not really in the same sense as people. Human emotion is highly complex. Grief often involves self-pity; anger tends to be laced with a desire for revenge. Yet an accurate picture of God's grief and God's anger must exclude such sinful responses. God's response is not tainted by corrupt elements.

When we deal with this metaphorical language in the Bible, we must remove the self-centeredness that is so often associated with these emotions.

This means that when we say "God loves," "God is angry," or "God is pleased," we must not unconsciously mix into these ideas the false elements that often characterize human love or anger or pleasure.

God is *not* an enlarged man.

With most metaphors, the author intended to make a comparison. There seem to be some situations, however, in which the writer used an *undesigned metaphor*. That is, his figurative language may be subconscious or unintentional.

The word "lord" (*kurios* in Greek) provides a good example of designed and undesigned metaphor. The literal meaning of this word, as found in Greek literature of the New Testament period, is "head" (as of a family) or "master" (as of a group). This is the meaning the disciples usually had in mind when they called Jesus "Lord."

Kurios is the Greek translation of the Hebrew word *adonay*. However, in the Old Testament, this word *adonay* is used both of God and of earthly masters. And quite often the term "the Lord God" is used. Furthermore, the covenant term for the God of Israel, *Yahweh*, was, like all Hebrew words, written in consonants only. The vowel points that were added to these consonants were the same as the vowels for the word Lord (*adonay*). The word *Yahweh* was considered by the Jews to be too sacred to pronounce. When they saw the word *Yahweh* in the text, they automatically substituted the word *adonay*. Thus the metaphorical meaning of the word *kurios*, translated from the Hebrew *adonay*, came to have an exalted meaning in Hebrew thought.

So it may be that when Jesus' disciples called Him "Lord," they intended no metaphor but used it in the sense of "master of the group." Nevertheless they were using an unconscious metaphor that suggested a link between Jesus and the covenant God of Israel. Later, as they came to understand more of Jesus' teaching, and particularly after His death and resurrection, they became aware of the metaphorical meaning of Lord and used it automatically to refer to the deity of Christ.

A good example of this changing of the word "lord" is illustrated by Peter's words as translated in *The New English Bible*. In the Matthew account of Peter on the Mount of Transfiguration, Peter said to Jesus, "Lord, how good it is that we are here" (Matt. 17:4). In Mark's account, the words read "Rabbi, how good it is that we are here" (Mark 9:5), and Luke records it as "Master, how good it is that we are here" (Luke 9:33). By comparing the three accounts, it is clear that Peter's use of the word "Lord" (as recorded in Matthew) refers to Him as master or head of the group.

However, in 1 Peter (written about A.D. 62–69, long after the death of Jesus), Peter writes, "But in your hearts reverence Christ as Lord" (1 Pet. 3:15), obviously referring to Christ as a sovereign ruler. The language in 1 Peter 3:14,15 is reminiscent of Isaiah 8:12,13 which refers to *Yahweh*, the covenant God of Israel. By this time, Peter's use of the word *kurios* to mean sovereign ruler was no longer metaphorical but literal. Or we might say it had changed from an unintentional metaphor to an intentional one.

We find the use of association in the Bible. This figure of speech is one in which two things are so closely associated that one automatically suggests the other. In the United States, "White House" has become a synonym for the President. The sentence, "The White House decided to release the speech earlier than usual," really refers to the President or those with his delegated authority. Substitutions like this are natural to our thinking and they were natural to the thinking of the writers of Scripture.

In Genesis 42, Jacob did not want Benjamin to go back to Egypt with his sons to purchase more food. If harm befell Benjamin on the way, Jacob said, "You would bring down my gray hairs with sorrow to Sheol" (v. 38). Here, gray hairs stand for "me, as an old man."

Paul used this kind of substitution with the terms "circumcision" and "uncircumcision." Romans 3:30 says, "He [God] will justify the circumcised on the ground of their faith and the uncircumcised through their faith." The context shows that "circumcised" stands for the Jews and "uncircumcised" stands for the Gentiles.

In other figures of speech, *a whole is used for a part or a part for a whole.* An individual may be used for a class of people, or a class for an individual. In Romans 1:16, Paul writes, "For I am not ashamed of the gospel: it is the power of God for salvation to every one who has faith, to the Jew first and also to the Greek." "The Jew" and "the Greek" obviously means the Jews and the Greeks.

Judges 12:7, *literally translated*, says: "And Jephthah judged Israel for six years. Then Jephthah, the Gileadite, died, and he was buried in the *cities* of Gilead."

74

Jephthah obviously could not be buried in more than *one* city. Why does the text read *cities?* Although Jephthah had served the interests of all the tribes of Israel, his own tribe *as a group* claimed his burial place. Most translators of this passage have added the words *one of* in italics before "the cities" to indicate an addition not in the original text. This figure of speech indicating *a group as one* underlines the strength of Israel's tribal ties.

One of the most picturesque examples of this figure of speech appears in Micah 4:3 and in Isaiah 2:4, "And they shall beat their swords into plowshares, and their spears into pruning hooks" (*KJV*). Both Micah and Isaiah picture the house of Jehovah as occupying a central place in the end times. All nations will stream to it. It offers instruction and makes important decisions affecting people everywhere. The abandonment of two weapons—swords and spears—stands for total disarmament.

The picture is reversed in Joel 3:10, which says, "Beat your plowshares into swords, and your pruning hooks into spears." This is far more dramatic than to say, "Arm yourselves for war; organize the people for military conflict."

These are all examples of *association* as a figure of speech.

The Bible is rich in poetic figures of personification. Almost everyone's imagination is quickened and responsive to the sharp imagery of the Bible. Jesus used personification many times. In Matthew 6:34, He says, "Therefore do not be anxious about tomorrow, for tomorrow will be anxious for itself." Anxiety is a quality of people, not of days or tomorrows; but by saying it this way, Jesus pictured the folly of torturing ourselves by unnecessary worry about the future.

The Psalms are full of vivid personifications. In Psalm 114, the psalmist celebrates God's delivery of the Jews from Egypt. He writes (in poetry)

"The sea looked and fled,
Jordan turned back.
The mountains skipped like rams,
The hills like lambs.

. . . .

Tremble, O earth, at the presence of the Lord,
at the presence of the God of Jacob."

(vv. 3,4,7)

Some Figures of Speech Are Not Fully Expressed

In English grammar, the term ellipsis refers to an idea that is not fully expressed. This form appears often in today's literature in sentences such as, "Cynical? Certainly. But also how bold and how refreshingly novel!" If this were written in full sentences it would read, "Is this cynical? Certainly it is. But also, how bold and how refreshingly novel it is." The first is just as clear and has an uncluttered swiftness lacking in the second. We do not consciously fill in the missing words, but we sense them intuitively.

The Scriptures also frequently use ellipses. However, because the original language is not our own and we do not share the writer's subconscious thought patterns, our intuitive sense does not fill in the missing sections.

The filling in is usually done by the translators after careful study of the context. The translators try to determine what the author meant by his sentence fragment and they fill it in for the reader. However, the Bible student must often judge for himself whether the expansion is what the original biblical writer would have said if he had done his own filling in, or whether he would be puzzled by the additions.

In Romans 7:24,25, we have an example of the kind of decisions translators must sometimes make about filling in ellipses. The *Revised Standard Version* reads: "Wretched man that I am! Who will deliver me from this body of death? Thanks be to God through Jesus Christ our Lord!" The *RSV* translators chose not to fill in the ellipsis occurring in verse 25.

The New Testament in Modern English (Phillips) chose to fill in: "It is an agonizing situation, and who on earth can set me free from the clutches of my own sinful nature? I thank God *there is a way out* through Jesus Christ our Lord" (italics added).

The New English Bible filled in the missing connection another way: "Miserable creature that I am, who is there to rescue me out of this body doomed to death? *God alone*, through Jesus Christ our Lord! Thanks be to God!" (italics added).

This kind of filling in accounts for some of the differences between translations. Another way of filling in Paul's ellipsis would be "Thanks be to God! *Deliverance comes* through Jesus Christ our Lord."

Understatement is often a powerful writing tool. Bible writers use understatement. One common form is known as *euphemism*—the substitution of a more indirect or delicate word for a blunt one that may be offensive or distasteful. We use a euphemism when we say "he passed away" rather than "he died."

Discussions in the Old Testament regarding sex are often done in euphemistic language. Leviticus 18:6, translated literally, reads "Every man of you shall not come near unto flesh of his flesh to uncover nakedness." Translators have clarified the first phrase "flesh of his flesh" and made it "near of kin" or "blood relatives." But the phrase "to uncover nakedness" is an Old Testament euphemism to designate sexual intercourse or to contract marriage. The passage in Leviticus is a warning against incest. The next few verses list specifically which relatives are included in the laws against incest.

Perhaps the right kind of euphemisms could be worth considering for our day. The language is direct enough so that the first readers, the Hebrew people, knew exactly what was being discussed. At the same time, there is no morbid preoccupation with details. The Old Testament is neither prudish nor prurient in dealing with sex. Euphemism helped achieve this.

Negation of the opposite is another form of understatement used in the Bible. This sounds more complex than it is. "Hailstorms are no rare occurrence here," actually means "Hailstorms are frequent here." This kind of figure occurs frequently in the Bible. First Thessalonians 2:15 (*KJV*) says, "Who both killed the Lord Jesus and their own prophets, and have persecuted us; *and they please not God*" (italics added). The translators of modern versions have usually discarded the understatement and given the direct form. The *RSV* translates the phrase, "Who killed both the Lord Jesus and the prophets, and drove us out, and displeased God." *Phillips* states, "Their present attitude is in opposition to both God and man." *New English Bible* reads, "Who are heedless of God's will."

Many pitfalls await the Bible student who does not recognize figures of hyperbole. Hyperbole, conscious exaggeration, is common in our own speech. We say laughingly, "I could kill you for that remark," when we really mean we are mildly annoyed by what was said. If a person says, "Man, after a day like this, I'm dead," we know he means, "I'm tired."

Hyperbole abounds in every language, including the language of the Bible. Jesus used it freely. He said: "If your right eye causes you to sin, pluck it out and throw it away; it is better that you lose one of your members than that your whole body be thrown into hell. And if your right hand causes you to sin, cut it off and throw it away" (Matt. 5:29,30).

No rational man chops off his hand or plucks out his eye. That hyperbole means that it is more important for a man to be whole and well spiritually than that he be whole and well physically; spiritual welfare must take precedence over physical welfare.

Unfortunately, not every instance of hyperbole is so easy to recognize. Matthew 5:32 says, "Every one who divorces his wife, except on the ground of unchastity, makes her an adulteress; and whoever marries a divorced woman commits adultery." Is this hyperbole? The answer is not easy and becomes a matter of interpretation and judgment. Whether we take it literally or as a degree of hyperbole, the message is still clear: marriage is sacred and God intends it to be permanent.

This passage should be considered with Matthew 5: 27,28, which also deals with adultery. Here Jesus said, "You have heard that it was said, 'You shall not commit adultery.' But I say to you that every one who looks [as a constant or customary activity] at a woman lustfully has already committed adultery with her in his heart." Is this hyperbole? Does Jesus actually mean that lustful looks are the equivalent of adultery in the eyes of God?

This example is given not to confuse the reader but to show how complex are the problems revolving around the interpretation of such simple figures of speech as the hyperboles used by Jesus.

In irony, the writer or speaker means the exact opposite of what the words say. If two friends meet on a blistering hot day and one says to the other, "I'm cool as a cucumber, Joe, how are you doing?" we recognize this as irony.

To the query, "How was the exam?" a student may reply, "You know Professor Smith. He always gives exams that are a snap." Yet the tone of voice indicates that he means exactly the opposite—that Professor Smith always gives very difficult exams and this one was no exception.

Irony is a vivid tool, but since we cannot hear the speaker the context is essential in recognizing irony in writing.

Jesus used irony effectively, but because we cannot hear the tone of voice in which He spoke, we sometimes fail to recognize it.

In Matthew 23, Jesus pronounced a long list of woes against the Pharisees, outlining in detail their previous sins and heaping scorn on their self-righteous claims that if they had been living in the days of their fathers, they would not have murdered the prophets as their ancestors did.

Then Jesus said, "Fill up, then, the measure of your fathers" (Matt. 23:32). This is irony. The Pharisees were bent on destroying Jesus. No miracles that Jesus did, no amount of teaching changed their attitude. Jesus is giving them up to their self-chosen destiny. With these words of irony, Jesus seals their fate: "Just keep right on with your sinning. Pretty soon you can cover all the sins your fathers missed." Obviously, Jesus was not baiting them or encouraging them to sin further by killing Him, but He was employing irony.

Paul also used irony. In 1 Corinthians 3 and 4, he discusses the partisan spirit at Corinth, where groups were aligning themselves as being for Paul or Apollos (see 1 Cor. 4:6). Their boasting about being in one group or another showed that they felt like proud possessors rather than receivers. So Paul adds a note of irony, "Already you are filled! Already you have become rich!

Without us you have become kings!" (1 Cor. 4:8). Paul used this method to strike out against their pride. The Corinthian Christians thought they were so rich in spiritual teaching that they could argue over which teacher was best. Paul adds, "Would that you did reign, so that we might share the rule with you!" He says that if this were only true, then he and the other apostles would be free from their sufferings and oppression. Paul used irony to show the gulf between the imaginary and the real.

Handling Figurative Language

1. Be alert for figurative language. It is not always easy to distinguish between the literal and the figurative, but if we place ourselves into the original setting we may be able to understand.

2. Reflect seriously on the literal meaning of the figure in its original setting. This makes it easier to recognize the relevant points of comparison and to make intelligent interpretations of figurative meanings.

3. Meditate on the reality to which the figurative language points. For example, Isaiah 59:1 reads, "The Lord's hand is not shortened, that it cannot save, or his ear dull, that it cannot hear." This figure points to God's infinite power to help deliver every person who calls upon Him. God has infinite capacity to hear, perceive and to understand what a person would like to say but cannot put into words (see Rom. 8:26).

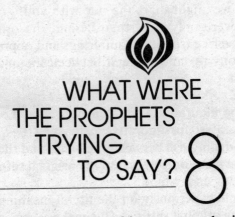

WHAT WERE THE PROPHETS TRYING TO SAY? 8

Understanding of prophecy hinges on two basic questions: What is a prophet? and what is prophecy?

Prophets are spokesmen for God who declare God's will to their people. But what did they actually do?

At first glance, prophets seem to play a more important role in the Old Testament than in the New. Old Testament prophets were superb proclaimers of the message of God. They set forth God's message both in promise and warning. They included both men and women—Deborah, Miriam, and Huldah are among the Old Testament prophets. They used drama, song, parable, story and exhortation. They were used by God to examine, prove, or test the people (see Jer. 6:27). They proclaimed inevitable judgment as well as judgment that could be avoided. They acted both as watchmen and as intercessors.

Prophets in the New Testament had much in common with the Old Testament prophets, although there were some differences. Peter viewed the gift of prophecy as coming upon both men and women and upon all age groups (see Acts 2:16–18) in fulfillment of the words of Joel. Paul encouraged the Christians at Corinth to strive for prophecy (see 1 Cor. 14).

The Purpose of Prophecy

Contrary to popular opinion, biblical prophecy was not primarily concerned with foretelling the future. In declaring God's will to the people, the prophet's message may have dealt with the past, the present, or the future. But the prophet always had one basic aim in mind—*to help the people know God as the most genuine reality that they could know and experience.* First Corinthians 14 says that prophecy involves upbuilding, encouragement, consolation, edification, conviction, conversion, and instruction. (This is sometimes called "forthtelling.")

Prophecy (especially the future aspects or "foretelling") had a comprehensive purpose. The prophet carried a message *from* God *to* his community *about* his community and about the nations surrounding his community and the world at large. The prophet himself usually was deeply involved in the life of that community. He did not speak as an outsider but as one intimately identified with those to whom he spoke.

In the Old Testament, the community was usually the theocracy of Israel, the people of God in the covenant nation. In the New Testament, the community was the church, the people of God of the new covenant.

Unfortunately, many persons today think of prophecy only in terms of foretelling future events. Prophetic "experts" today sometimes ignore those parts of the passages they are discussing that deal with the past or the present and concentrate on the future. And the more future the better! Some try to read a prophecy about jet airplanes into certain Old Testament passages to show how far ahead of his time the prophet was! This kind of thinking piles confusion on confusion concerning the nature of the prophet's message.

Every item of predictive prophecy was given to a particular historical people to awaken and stir them to righteousness by revealing in part what God will do in the future. Any disclosure of the future was given *to influence present action.* Probably the only way a description of a jet airplane could have influenced people's actions during Old Testament times would have been to increase their age-long desire to fly as a bird, or to make them more fearful of the military use of such a machine.

Predictive prophecy was never given to satisfy man's curiosity about the future. The future aspect of prophecy was intended to instruct, to reprove, to encourage, to call people to repentance. The New Testament often uses phrases such as "behold the days are coming when," and "in those days." Such passages show that God's program moves forward according to His schedule. He is acting. Throughout the Bible runs the theme that there will be many crises followed by a mighty climax when the age to come will break through in its totality. God will then reign supreme. His will is to be done on earth as it is in heaven.

Two Erroneous Views of Prophecy

Two erroneous views have risen in recent years that have gained a surprising number of adherents. The first erroneous view is that *predictive prophecy is a vivid way of writing history.* This view is held by many who assume that real prediction is impossible in a universe governed wholly by cause and effect. Those who hold this view insist that God never revealed objective truths

84

about Himself; He simply revealed Himself in events that would mean nothing to a person lacking faith.

However, there is much biblical material that the average prudent man would understand to be predictive prophecy and these predictions do not fit into a totally rationalistic world view. So the purveyors of this theory say that most of the apparently predictive materials were really written *after* the events they predict. Since history is rather dull to many readers, the prophetic style was used to liven up the narrative and make it more readable. If this strategy did not seem logical for certain prophetic messages, those messages were generalized and called a brilliant insight by a prophet whose mind refused to be shut up within the confines of Hebrew daily life. This is part of the reason some critics date some books of the Old Testament very late. They *had* to be written after the events they described to support the theory of the scholar.

But there are serious weaknesses in this view. Ordinary historical material in the Bible is not enigmatic like prophecy. It deals with many details and follows a basic chronological pattern. In contrast, the predictive prophetic narratives do not give subordinate details in any consistent train of thought or in developed time sequences. Any man who could write history in the form of Hebrew prophecy would have to forget half of what he knew in order to give the appearance of being a prophet, and the artificiality of such a tactic could not be hidden.

The second erroneous view is at the opposite extreme. The idea that *predictive prophecy is history written in advance* is just as erroneous as the idea that it is history written after the event. And it is wrong for somewhat the same reason. Predictive prophecy is enigmatic. It never gives enough details so that the prophetic sketch can be substituted for a historical summary.

Assume for a moment that the circle below contains all the elements or facts needed to give an adequate picture of a definite historical event. Each "x" represents one of these elements.

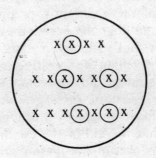

Some of the x's are circled; these represent the facts in a historical event that were revealed beforehand to and by the prophet. It is obvious that these alone would give a very inadequate picture. But if prophecy were simply history written beforehand, all of the x's would be circled and the enigmatic character of predictive prophecy would disappear.

For example, Matthew 4:14 says that the prophet Isaiah foretold Jesus' Galilean ministry. The Isaiah passage reads: "In the former time he brought into contempt the land of Zebulun and the land of Naphtali, but in the latter time he will make glorious the way of the sea, the land beyond the Jordan, Galilee of the nations.

"The people who walked in darkness
    have seen a great light;
    those who dwelt in a land of deep darkness,
    on them has light shined" (Isa. 9:1,2).

"The way of the sea" meant the ancient caravan route that ran from Damascus to the Mediterranean. "Beyond the Jordan" referred to the land on the east side of the Jordan and the Sea of Galilee. "Galilee of the nations" was the northern borders of upper and lower Galilee and was singled out as that part of the land that had been especially dishonored, but at a later time would be honored. A people whose course of action was in darkness (the Gentiles) would see great light.

These words were fulfilled during the ministry of Jesus. Then why was it not history written beforehand? Because the *historical* record of the New Testament must be read to see just where Jesus carried on His ministry in Galilee and in what sense "the people who walked in darkness saw a great light."

The Gospels show that the Galilean ministry of Jesus was largely limited to His own Jewish people. He was the light that shone brightly in the darkness of *His own people.*

During His early ministry, only a few Gentiles came into contact with Him. However, through the ministry of the early Church, many Gentiles did come to see the great light that illumined their darkness.

Prophecy cannot be history written beforehand because God does not disclose enough of the major and minor elements that are essential for even an incomplete historical picture. What God makes known as well as what He withholds are both a part of the total plan of redemption. As history moves on, the full-orbed picture emerges. Earlier intimations of what is to come remind us that all of history is in God's sovereign control.

How Prophets Received Their Messages

How do we know that the prophets actually receivd their messages from God? Would it not be possible for prophets to pretend they had received a divine message, when in reality they were making it up to have a position of prominence among the people? Or was the prophet self-deluded, thinking that he or she was a messenger of God, when in reality it was hallucinations or mental illness?

There *are* such prophets in the Scriptures. Jeremiah 14:14, says: "And the Lord said to me: 'The prophets are prophesying lies in my name; I did not send them, nor did I command them or speak to them. They are prophesying to you a lying vision, worthless divination, and the deceit of their own minds.' "

Such prophets created their own material without any genuine relationship with God. In one sense, the true prophets also created their own material, for each one's individual style is stamped on his message, but they did not originate their messages. They stood in a vital relationship to God and it was God who spoke as well as the prophets.

But how did the prophets receive their messages?

Occasionally God used dreams or night visions to reveal Himself. Paul saw in a dream the man of Macedonia saying, "Come over to Macedonia and help us" (Acts 16:9). The dreams or visions seem to be the ordinary dreams of the night, with the power to retain what was dreamed. It does not follow, of course, that *our* dreams are revelations of God!

Many of the messages came when the prophets were in an ecstatic state. This was not a self-induced excitement in which the prophet jumped around in an irrational manner. Rather, it was a condition in which the prophet's mental and spiritual faculties rose to a new level of performance.

The prophet Habakkuk tells of stationing himself on a tower to *see* what God would say to him. He was alert and prepared for God to reveal something to him. Most of such ecstatic experiences occurred in the daytime—

only a few at night. The best modern analogy to an ecstatic vision might be closed circuit television. The prophet is sometimes said to "see" the word or message of the Lord (see Isa. 2:1; Mic. 1:1). In other passages, the prophets saw a vision, an utterance, oracle, or revelation (see Isa. 1:1; Ezek. 1:1; 13:16).

The visions that were actually from God were *content-centered*. The passage in Jeremiah shows what the Lord *did not do* for false prophets. The false prophets "are prophesying lies in my name; I did not send them, nor did I command them or speak to them. They are prophesying to you a lying vision, worthless divination, and the deceit of their own minds" (14:14).

By reversing this we can see what the Lord *did do* for true prophets. The implication is that the true prophets are sent by God. He does command them; He does speak to them; they prophesy visions of truth.

Another way in which God reveals His message to His prophets is through direct communication. In dreams and ecstatic visions, the prophet apparently sees or hears as if he were seeing and hearing a motion picture. In direct encounter there is no dream or vision, but rather a direct communication from God to the prophet.

This occurred many times in the Old Testament. One classic example is that of Isaiah's message to King Hezekiah, recorded in 2 Kings 20:1-6. Hezekiah was very ill. Isaiah came to him with a message from God that he was going to die. Hearing this, Hezekiah prayed fervently, asking the Lord to remember that he was a king who had faithfully served God. Isaiah left Hezekiah after delivering the message of impending death. On his way out of the palace, Isaiah met God, "And before Isaiah had gone out of the middle court, the word of the Lord came to him" (2 Kings 20:4). Isaiah was told to go back and tell Hezekiah that God would heal him and give him 15 additional years, and that Jerusalem would be delivered from the oppression of the king of Assyria.

Isaiah did not have a vision or dream. He had a direct message from God. He was awake, fully alert, and active.

Prophets Were Involved in Events

Often in the Bible, prophets were deeply involved in specific historical events of their day. As a result of this involvement, the prophet came into a relationship with God and received an authoritative message to deliver.

It was a time of severe crisis when King Jehoiakim burned up the scroll produced at the command of God by Jeremiah and his secretary, Baruch (Jer. 36:1-32). The king ordered Jeremiah and Baruch to be taken prisoners, but God hid them. Then the word of the Lord came to Jeremiah again. He was to prepare another scroll like the one the king had burned. He reproduced the first book and added many like words. Included in the second prophecy was the news that Jehoiakim would be slain and he would not even have the honor of being buried.

Another personal involvement is recorded in Jeremiah 41:1—43:7. After many of the leaders of Judah were deported to Babylon, the king of Babylon appointed Gedaliah to govern those remaining in Palestine. Gedaliah was murdered and the remaining leaders feared reprisals. They asked Jeremiah what to do and promised that they would obey whatever the Lord told them. Jeremiah had to wait 10 days before he received the answer from the Lord: if they would stay in the land of Palestine, God would establish them; if they went to Egypt, they would be blotted out. Even as Jeremiah delivered the message, he sensed that his hearers had already made up their minds. They all fled to Egypt despite the prophecy. Furthermore, they took Jeremiah and Baruch with them. The prophet was clearly involved with the events about which he prophesied.

Although the prophet spoke from God, he spoke as a man within a people to a people. He was not an outsider looking in. He was an insider—one with the people to whom he ministered and about whom he prophesied. He understood his message and many of its implications.

Prophets Had Restricted Perspective

When God spoke to and through His servants in predictive prophecy, He did not give them unlimited vision. Instead, they were confined within a divinely limited perspective.

This is clear regarding the second coming of Christ. Most of the writers of the New Testament indicate they believed that Christ would come during their own lifetime. John in Revelation repeats this over and over. In Revelation 3:11, Christ declares, "I am coming at once (without delay)" (literal translation). This appears three times in chapter 22—in verses 7,12, and 20.

But two thousand years have gone by and Christ still has not returned. This long interval, however, does not change the great issues that confront people in every generation. If we believe that the return of Christ and the consummation of history may occur in our lifetime, we become more alive to the significant issues that we face. Each generation faces its own set of issues. How seriously we consider them shows whether God is a reality to us and whether we believe the climax of history is a genuine possibility.

The New Testament writers believed Christ was returning to this earth to change it. Their belief was not a form of escapism. They believed that Christ's presence would break the hold that sin has on men.

91

Prophets Spoke in Their Own Language

The language of the prophets is colored by all of their present and past experiences. The prophet spoke to his or her people in their thought patterns and in their language because these were the language and thought patterns they knew.

To them transportation meant horses, chariots, camels, boats. Armaments meant spears, shields, swords. Worship usually meant the Temple and sacrifices. The enemies of God were the Philistines, Moabites, Babylonians, and others.

The prophets' historical situations affected the predictive aspect of their messages. Some predictions dealt with the immediate future. Others looked down vast corridors of time, although the prophets themselves may not have realized that. They looked for the soon end of the present order and the beginning of the age to come. God limited their perspective so that they and the people to whom they ministered would be God-centered—not event-centered.

When the prophets touched upon events that may even yet be unfulfilled, their language is puzzling because their descriptive imagery is foreign to us. Thankfully, their main emphasis is on God rather than on events. When events are put in the foreground, people tend to put God in the background. This is a form of idolatry.

How do interpreters handle the language of predictive prophecy whose fulfillment is a long way from the time of the prophet and may be yet to come? There have been three common methods.

Some interpreters expect literal fulfillment in all details. If the prophet mentions horses and bridles, some interpreters look for horses and bridles. If the prophet mentions shields, bucklers, bows and arrows, they believe that these are the weapons that will be used. This approach becomes a bit ludicrous when applied to today or the future and it shows that the interpreter has forgotten the perspective of the prophet and the people to whom he ministered. The prophet talked to his people in the only language they knew and the only language he knew. When they thought of weapons, it was spears and shields that came to mind.

Other interpreters apply a symbolic meaning to the prophecy. These interpreters make predictive prophecy a picture of the hopes of the prophets for a better life. They apply a prophetic picture to the Christian Church, letting it cover part or all of the period from the beginning of the Church to the New Jerusalem of Revelation 21,22.

Many interpreters think in terms of equivalents, analogy or correspondence. This is the approach preferred by the writers of this book. In this method, the chariots of the prophet's day will have an equivalent at the time of its fulfillment. The enemies of the people of God in one period are replaced by later enemies. The details of worship of God's people at an earlier period will be replaced by modes of worship of God during the period of fulfillment.

This principle of equivalents can be illustrated by examining the prophecy of Ezekiel in Ezekiel 40—48. Ezekiel prophesied that worship of God was to be restored. The prophet gave elaborate specifications as to the exact size of the Temple, floor plans, symbols to be employed, the kinds of sacrifices to be conducted there and their order; the kind of garments the priests were to wear; whom they were to marry; what they were to teach the people, and how the land was to be divided among the people of Israel.

Where was Ezekiel when he received and delivered

this prophecy? He and all the other Israelites were in exile in Babylon. There was no Temple at all, no priesthood, no ritual. Nor has Ezekiel's prophecy been fulfilled up to the present day.

What does this mean? None of us can say positively. But the message brought by Ezekiel to his people was greatly encouraging. It meant to those lonely exiled people that the worship of God was not past. God would ultimately triumph and the knowledge of Him would never perish from the earth.

But what about this specific prophecy? Was it all a mistake? Or could Ezekiel's description of the worship of God by His people still be fulfilled in the day when Christ returns to bring the consummation of the age?

Perhaps. But in the light of God's action in Jesus Christ, the fulfillment can hardly be literal. How could the true worship of God by the people of God return to the sacrifices that were abolished by the supreme sacrifice of Christ? The rituals of which Ezekiel spoke were but a shadow that was fulfilled in Christ. This is a place for the principle of equivalents.

The 12 tribes suggest the unity of the people of God—Jews and Gentiles—in Christ. (Compare Ezek. 43:7–9 with Rev. 7:9,15.)

The Temple, ritual and priests were all involved in the worship of God, in bringing men into vital fellowship with God. The book of Hebrews says that with Christ as our High Priest, all older commandments regarding the priesthood were annulled (Heb. 7:12–28). The factors of which Ezekiel spoke were the shadow of which Jesus Christ is the reality. The coming worship will exalt Jesus Christ.

The division of land among the 12 tribes of Israel, discussed by Ezekiel, may reveal the perfect justice that Christ will bring when He returns. All past rivalries and inequities will go. God's people—now including Jews and Gentiles—will be under Christ's command to bring about a whole new epoch.

Ezekiel's thinking in these chapters was focused by God on a great reality. He used the language of his day and the worship forms familiar to his readers to make his message understandable to them. Those of us who have his language plus all of the New Testament can still see only dimly the great glory yet to come!

Understanding Prophecy

1. Analyze the passage in terms of history, context, and the literal meaning of the words and their relationship to each other. Understand as much as possible about the historical situation of the prophet and of the people to whom he ministers. Read carefully what precedes and what follows the particular passage being studied. Consult any parallel passage that may shed light. However, don't be surprised to find that prophetic passages are not usually arranged in any systematic order!

2. Note exactly to whom or to what the passage refers. Is the prophecy addressed to readers or hearers and is it also *about* those same readers or hearers? Or is it about someone else? Does it have any qualifications attached? Is it an "if these people do this thing, this will happen"?

If the prophecy has *forthtelling*, what was the people's condition and how did they respond?

If the prophecy has *foretelling*, was it fulfilled or not? If it was fulfilled, study the writings that tell about the fulfillment. Some predictive prophecies, although referring to one specific event, may have additional applications. For example, Daniel 11 tells about the coming desecration of the Temple: "Forces from him shall appear and profane the temple and fortress, and shall take away the continual burnt offering. And they shall set up the abomination that makes desolate" (Dan. 11:31).

This was fulfilled in the revolting acts of Antiochus Epiphanes IV (170–168 B.C.) when he desecrated the Temple in Jerusalem, slaughtered thousands of Jews and finally set up a Greek altar to Zeus in the place where the altar for burnt offerings had once stood.

However, Jesus used the Daniel prophecy to refer to another event when He spoke in Matthew 24:15, "So when you see the desolating sacrilege spoken of by the prophet Daniel, standing in the holy place (let the reader understand). . . ." Jesus was referring to the fall of Jerusalem that was to occur in A.D. 70. The words may also describe the military situation in Palestine and Jerusalem at the time when Christ shall return.

Paul uses similar language to describe the man of sin, the final Antichrist: "For that day will not come, unless the rebellion comes first, and the man of lawlessness is revealed, the son of perdition, who opposes and exalts himself against every so-called god or object of worship, so that he takes his seat in the temple of God, proclaiming himself to be God" (2 Thess. 2:3,4).

Multiple applications of the prophetic language can and do occur. The message is real but it is also elastic.

3. Distinguish between direct and typological prediction, especially when fulfillment of Old Testament prophecy is found in the New Testament.

Direct prediction means that an Old Testament prophetic statement is fulfilled solely in New Testament times. For example, Micah 5:2 states that Christ would be born at Bethlehem. The fulfillment is seen in Matthew 2:5, 6.

A *typological* prediction is an Old Testament statement that referred to something in Old Testament times, but had its highest application of meaning in the events, people, or message of the New Testament. In Zechariah 11:12,13, the prophet Zechariah is acting as a shepherd for His people, serving as God's watchman for them. In the prophecy, Zechariah is "bought off" by the people for 30 pieces of silver, which he casts into the treasury of God's house. Matthew quotes this passage (Matt. 26:15) in reference to the price paid to Judas for the betrayal of Jesus. Such typological prediction is common throughout the New Testament. To understand it, we must be well acquainted with both Old and New Testament contexts where the material is found.

4. God's ultimate revelation of Himself in Christ colors all earlier revelations. We look at the Old Testament through the eye of the Christian—not through the eye of the Old Testament Jew. Christ spoke of one flock and one shepherd at the climax of His earthly ministry (John 10:16). We belong to this one flock, the Church, Christ's body. Jesus Christ forever broke down the barrier between Jews and Gentiles. The household of God is a living organism, tied to Jesus Christ. It includes believers from both the Old Covenant and the New Covenant. God has a great destiny for His people, since the new covenant is an everlasting covenant (Heb. 13:20).

5. Apocalyptic imagery is difficult to handle. The term "apocalyptic" refers to those portions of the Bible in which the writer paints a dark picture of imminent disaster or cosmic cataclysm is which God destroys the ruling powers of evil and brings forth ultimate righteousness. There is a dark background with a bright ending. The books of Daniel, Zechariah, and Revelation have large portions of such material and other books have smaller amounts. In reading apocalyptic imagery, we must follow the basic principle involved in understanding all figurative language. Would our interpretation of

this difficult imagery have made sense to the original readers of the material? It is much better to say, "I don't know what this means," than to force a meaning that the imagery was not meant to carry. These problems will be discussed further in the next chapter on the language of creation and climax.

6. How do we know what is literal and what is figurative in prophetic materials? The very words "literal" and "figurative" are often misunderstood. By literal we mean the customary and socially acknowledged meaning of the word. By figurative we mean a higher application of the literal meaning (i.e., he was "fishing" for an answer).

The figurative meaning of a term or a passage must be based on its literal meaning. The literal meaning should not be abandoned except for good reasons based on the immediate context or the larger context of Scripture. Unfortunately, interpreters often choose figurative interpretations of certain passages simply to make them fit into the rest of their theological or eschatological schemes.

What the original readers would have thought about the passage must be constantly considered. We must also examine pertinent New Testament teaching. Occasionally the original readers (and perhaps even the writers) were wrong in what they concluded. For example, Paul and the early Church obviously thought that the return of Christ would come within their own lifetimes. God chose to limit their perspective in this regard, and the perspective of each Christian through the centuries since then has been similarly limited. But knowing this, we now have good reason to interpret some of these passages with a less literal approach.

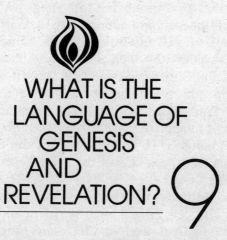

WHAT IS THE LANGUAGE OF GENESIS AND REVELATION? 9

Probably no chapters of the Bible have elicited more intense emotion and disagreement than those involving the creation of the world and its climax or culmination. Unfortunately, the heat of the discussions has rarely generated much light.

The basic question usually is: How literal or how figurative should be our interpretation of the Scriptures that deal with these subjects? The question is *"How literal?"* or *"How figurative?"* *not* "Shall we be literal or shall we be figurative?" For the person who shouts the loudest for a "literal" interpretation nearly always has some figurative elements, and the one who espouses the "figurative" cause must base his meanings on literal elements.

For example, the story of creation of man as recorded

in Genesis 1 and 2 says that God "breathed into his nostrils the breath of life; and man became a living being." It states that God "walked in the garden in the cool of the day" and He "made for Adam and his wife garments of skins, and clothed them."

A strictly literal approach to this picture would demand that God be a being with lungs who knelt beside the form of man and administered a kind of mouth-to-mouth artificial respiration. It would demand a God who has feet with which to walk, and hands with which to sew. But Christ said that "God is spirit, and those who worship him must worship in spirit and truth" (John 4:24). Paul said, "[God] alone has immortality and dwells in unapproachable light, whom no man has ever seen or can see" (1 Tim. 6:16). How can the account in Genesis and the words of the New Testament both be "literally" true?

The interpreter who wants to make everything figurative is also caught in a bind. If Adam and Eve and the fall are all figurative—is there any literal event, any historical occurrence, to which they point? If sin is a reality, how is it related to the story of Genesis? Has man always been at odds with God? Did man break off a harmonious relationship? These are problems that have concerned Christians for generations.

Figures of Speech Common in Jewish Thought

A careful study of the Bible shows that figures of speech are deeply woven into the fabric of Jewish thought. Ancient people did not think or talk in abstractions as we often do. Early people used figures of speech drawn from their everyday agricultural and pastoral life.

In talking about God, one of the biblical writers' most frequent figures of speech is the anthropomorphism. This means that the physical qualities of man are used to describe God. Each writer knew that God did not have hands or feet or lungs. But he also knew that God had created man in a sense similar to that in which a potter forms or molds a container, and that God made it possible for him to "breathe" or live. The writer knew that God cares for the physical needs of people in the sense that a tailor clothes a man. He knew that Adam and Eve could commune with God somewhat as a person talks with another person in a garden.[1]

It is important to remember the distinction between figurative and literal. It is not that literal means "true" while figurative means "make-believe." A figurative meaning may be more "true" than the literal meaning. The term literal refers to the customary meaning of a word in an ordinary earthly situation. Figurative refers to the transfer of this ordinary meaning by analogy or comparison to show a different or deeper truth.

Sometimes a figurative meaning becomes more common than the literal one. If we say, "He is a windbag," we do not mean that he is wind tied up in a bag. However, we rarely use the term windbag except in a figurative way. That bit of figurative language may depict an accurate picture of the man—or it may be entirely false.

Our aim is to arrive at the meaning that the original writer had in mind and to find the truth that this has for us in our day.

To say that certain language is figurative does not mean that the event is unreal. Figurative language may be the most accurate way of conveying what is real, abiding, and certain. Any human language used to describe events that took place or will take place in a sphere of existence which no human has observed is by its very nature figurative. No man was present at creation; climax is yet to take place. Any account of these events would have to be written in language based on

101

the known or experienced phenomena of the writer. How else could any meaning be conveyed?

Creation Account Is Pre-Scientific

The language of the creation account is pre-scientific and is directed to those who knew nothing of the vastness of space, the world of the microscope, or the intricacies of physical organisms. Most people still know little about these things. Any pride in our superior scientific knowledge is ridiculous when we consider the vast areas about which science still knows little or nothing.

If the Bible had been written in the scientific language of our day, it would have been meaningless to all who preceded us and it would be meaningless to generations yet to come who will develop vocabulary and concepts unknown to us. The accounts could only be written within the framework and cosmology of people of that day. It is popular pre-scientific language.

God as the Ultimate Cause

In dealing with passages about creation or climax it is necessary to remember that the writers did not discuss "how"; they did not concern themselves with secondary causes and effects, but focused on God as the ultimate cause.

Unfortunately, we keep asking *how* God did this or that, and *how* God will accomplish something in the future, rather than giving our primary attention to the clearly stated fact that God did it or will do it.

Events Not Always Chronological

The biblical narratives dealing with creation are written in the style and with the outlook of ancient man. This means, among other things, that events are not necessarily recounted in chronological order. This is true of many parts of the Old Testament. In the book of Jeremiah, the writer starts with events during the reign of one king, then moves to another king, and then comes back to the first king. Chronology was not as important to ancient writers as it is to us.

Poetic sequence, or subject matter, or logic, or some other factor often dominated the choice of arrangement rather than chronology. Without understanding this, even a grade-school child may be confused by the Genesis account in which light was created on the "first day" while the sun is not made until the "fourth day."

Certain Numbers Had Symbolic Meaning

The use of certain symbolic numbers had great importance to ancient people. *The number seven appears symbolically in the writings not only of the Jews but of all Semites.* It seems to signify a fullness or totality. To the Jews, it symbolized a totality designed and ordained by God.

The number seven played an important part in the religious ritual of Jews and in their means of recounting history.

In Genesis 10, the names in the generations of Noah total 70—a "full" picture of the nations of the world. In Numbers 11:16, Moses appoints 70 elders over the people of Israel. In Exodus 1:5 we are told that "all the offspring of Jacob were seventy persons." In Genesis 4:24, Cain was avenged sevenfold and Lamach 70 times seven.

The story of a boy who was brought back to life by Elisha is recounted in 2 Kings 4:35. It says that the boy sneezed seven times—an indication that life had fully returned.

This use of seven and its multiples is also prominent in the New Testament. The story of the seven brothers who successively married the same woman is obviously meant to give Jesus the idea of an extensive series (Matt. 22:23–32).

In Matthew 1, the genealogy of Joseph lists three series of fourteen generations. Matthew's selection does not coincide with the Old Testament genealogies, but he apparently chose names to be included in his genealogy so that they would come out in a series of three fourteens. This may have been a memory device, or the desire to use a multiple of seven, or a combination of both.

Jesus used the example of the man who was to be forgiven not seven times but 70 times seven—continually and fully forgiven. In Luke 10:1, Jesus is said to send out 70 disciples.

Symbolic use of the number seven comes to much fuller play in the book of Revelation in telling the climax of history. The book is addressed to seven churches (1:4); and speaks of seven spirits before God's throne (1:4); seven lampstands (1:12); seven stars (1:16); seven seals (5:1) seven trumpets and seven angels (8:2); seven thunders (10:3); seven heads and seven crowns (12:3; 13:1; 17:3); seven bowls of wrath (16:1); a lamb that has seven horns and seven eyes (5:6). The beast (dragon) has seven heads (12:3)—perhaps to indicate the full development of the forces hostile to God.

The use of seven as a symbolic number is extensive in the Bible. Why did the number seven gain this great significance? We cannot be sure, of course, but perhaps seven appeared significant to ancient man in his then observable cosmos and its order. He probably found his first basis of reckoning time and dividing time by observing the four phases of the moon in seven-day periods. Thus a "week" became his first measurable unit of time beyond the sunrise and sunset that marked a day.

How natural that the writer of Genesis should use a seven-day literary framework as his symbolic unit to describe the completion of a cataclysmic, significant event! It is likely that the early readers or listeners of the account understood the use of this literary framework far better than readers of more recent generations—especially of Western civilization.

This use of a seven-day literary framework is also found in early literature outside the Bible. The Canaanites had a story about a palace to their god Baal being erected in seven days—although it would have been impossible for a palace to be constructed with primitive building methods in seven days. It was simply a number indicating the completion of an important event that took an indefinite period of time.

This is only one illustration of the fact that ancient peoples' patterns of thought and ways of expressing ideas were very different from twentieth-century Western modes. Unless we make strenuous efforts to understand the early framework, culture, and thought patterns, we may grossly misinterpret what these ancient writings are saying.

The creation story appears in a Hebrew framework of seven days. The week is divided into two three-day periods.

Genesis 1:2 describes the earth as "without form and void." The Hebrew phrase is *Tohu wa-bohu*. The phrase itself has a poetic ring. *Tohu* means unformed and *bohu* means empty or unfilled.

During the first half (three days) of the six-day work week, God remedied the "formless" aspect of the earth by acts of dividing. On the first "day" He divided the light from darkness. On the second "day" God divided the "lower waters" from the "upper waters." (The ancients thought of the "firmament" or "heavens" not as space but as a solid substance, so that the "firmament" formed a sort of canopy over the earth. Today this is called atmosphere.) On the third "day" God divided the lower waters from the dry land and also covered the earth with vegetation.

In the last three "days" of work, God "filled" the emptiness or void of the earth, according to the Hebrew writer. The work of these last three days follows the same pattern as that of the first three.

On the fourth "day" God created the sun, moon, and stars. This corresponds to the first day's activity of separating light from darkness.

The fifth "day" God filled the "lower waters" with fish, and sea creatures, and the "upper waters" with birds. The dividing of the "upper and lower waters" had been made on the second "day."

On the sixth "day" God filled the land that had been "formed" on the "third day." On it He placed animals and man and told man that the vegetation that had been created on the third day was food for him and the animals.

Day-Forming by dividing	Day-Filling by making
1. Light from darkness	4. Sun, moon, stars
2. Upper waters from lower waters	5. Fish and birds
3. Land from seas (and creation of vegetation)	6. Animals and man

Looking at the Genesis account from this perspective, it appears that it is written within a literary framework rather than a chronological or scientific framework. This in no way lessens the great truths that the creation account has for us.

The Genesis account corrects common philosophical and theological errors. First, it teaches clearly that God and nature are not identical. The pantheist gains no comfort or help from Genesis. It teaches that God is above and separate from the universe. He is the Creator.

Second, it teaches that there is *one* God—not one among many.

Third, it teaches that God is good and that everything He made was good.

Fourth, it teaches that God moved in an orderly way from a chaotic situation to one of form and beauty. Creation did not do this by itself.

Vocabulary of Creation and Climax

The Hebrew language was rich, capable of many nuances of meaning. It was highly pictorial, built on the agricultural and pastoral life of the people. The early Hebrews, like every generation before or since, were largely enclosed within their own mode of life and their language reflected that mode. Ideas can be portrayed only in language known to the writers or speakers. Therefore, the language of the writers' experience was used to describe the distant past, the distant future, and eternal abiding realities as they understood them.

The biblical picture of heaven is expressed in terms of the palaces and riches of earthly potentates. Gold, jewels, rich robes, crowns, thrones—these signified the epitome of splendor on earth. How natural, then, that the splendors of heaven should be described in such terms. The people of that day were probably more aware of the symbolic nature of their use of language than today's readers sometimes are. However, it might be very difficult for generations far removed from us to tell by our writings how figurative was our use of words.

To illustrate the extent of the language problem involved in the creation and climax accounts, let us take one passage that shows the complexities of vocabulary. Genesis 2:7,8 says: "Then the Lord God formed man of dust from the ground, and breathed into his nostrils the breath of life; and man became a living being. And the Lord God planted a garden in Eden, in the east; and there he put the man whom he had formed."

In this passage we have the terms "formed," "breathed," "breath of life," and "living being." These show the complications of vocabulary.

The verb here for "formed" is the Hebrew word *yatzar*, which means to form or fashion. The participle of this verb is used in Jeremiah 18:4–6 to describe a potter forming a vessel. The potter is spoken of as the one forming. When this idea is applied to God, the figurative meaning is immediately apparent. God does not have hands to handle clay as the potter does. But this language gives a more personal feeling than the more abstract word "create." It indicates the personal involvement of God as "the one forming."

What did God "form" or "mold"? In Genesis 2:7,8, He formed or molded man. In verse 19 the same word is used of animals, "So out of the ground the Lord God *formed* every beast of the field and every bird of the air."

Apparently God used the same materials to form man, birds and animals—"out of the ground." This seems to indicate what common sense and science have long since confirmed—that the physical elements of man, birds and beasts have a common base.

This common base has been a great boon to medical science. It makes possible, for example, for insulin from a cow to be used by a person with diabetes, permitting that person to live a full and useful life. After death, man, beasts and birds all return to "dust" as is stated with remarkable simplicity in Genesis 3:19, "You are dust, and to dust you shall return."

In Isaiah 44:1,2, and 24 there is a figure of speech

108

involving the word *yatzar* "to form." Verses 1 and 2 state:

> "But now hear, O Jacob my servant, Israel whom I have chosen! Thus says the Lord who made you, who formed you from the womb and will help you."

The first verse shows that the passage refers to the nation Israel. The figure of speech is that of a child growing in its mother's womb, and the figure refers to God's forming of the people of Israel. Both the figure (the growth of a fetus in the uterus) and the history of Israel indicate that this "forming" was a process that continued over a period of time. In fact, in Isaiah's time, God was still forming or fashioning the nation even though more than a thousand years had passed since He had first called Abraham to be the father of a great multitude. In Isaiah 43:1, the verb *barah* (to create) is used as a synonym for the verb *yatzar* (to form) in a typical case of Hebrew poetic parallelism:

"But now thus says the Lord,	*literally*
he who created you, O Jacob;	the one creating you, O Jacob;
he who formed you, O Israel."	the one forming you, O Israel.

The "creation" of Jacob obviously was no instantaneous process involving making something out of nothing. The active participle in Hebrew, which is used here, *boracká*, indicates a person or thing conceived as being in the continual uninterrupted exercise of an activity.[2]

A passage in Jeremiah 10:12,13 uses the active participle to picture God as both creator and sustainer of the universe:

> "It is he who made the earth by his power [participle, literally 'was making'], who estab-

109

lished the world by his wisdom [participle, literally 'was establishing'], and by his understanding stretched out the heavens. When he utters his voice there is a tumult of waters in the heavens, and he makes the mist rise from the ends of the earth. He makes lightnings for the rain, and he brings forth the wind from his storehouses" [participle, literally 'he is bringing forth'].

In Jeremiah 10:16, the writer says that creation shows the God of the Bible to be distinct from all idols—ancient or modern:

"Not like these [idols] is he who is the portion of Jacob, for he is the one who formed all things [participle, literally 'the one who is forming the sum total of all that exists'], and Israel is the tribe of his inheritance; the LORD of hosts is his name."

These passages and others like them indicate that God is personally involved not only in the creation of the world but also in its daily operation. The creation of the world involved process, and God continues the process of its daily operation. Yet God's personal involvement in the thunderstorm does not mean that secondary causes, such as high pressure centers, are not at work.

The next terms that are complex in meaning are "breathed" and "breath of life." "Then the Lord God formed man of dust from the ground, and *breathed* into his nostrils the *breath of life;* and man became a living being" (italics added).

Breath is used often in the Bible to symbolize or indicate a living creature. For example, Job maintains that he will not be guilty of falsehood nor will he utter deceit as long as his *breath* is in him (see Job 27:3).

Obviously, it was the impartation of life and the resulting function of breathing that is referred to in Genesis 2:7, "Then the Lord God formed man of dust from the ground, and breathed into his nostrils the breath of life; and man became a living being."

The third term, "living being" (Hebrew *nefesh chayyah*), used in Genesis 2:7, refers to man. However, it is also used in Genesis 2:19 and refers to animals, "And whatever the man called every living creature (*nefesh chayyah*), that was its name."

The same term also appears in Genesis 1:20,21,24,30 in describing the fish, birds, and animals. It appears in Genesis 9:12,15 in reference to the covenant that God made with Noah and his sons and with "every living creature."

Some people have tried to maintain that the term "living being" in Genesis 2:7 refers to man's eternal soul, but a study of the use of the word in other contexts rules this out—unless one is willing to say that every fish, bird, and animal also has an eternal soul.

Actually, the description of man as a "living being" shows man's likeness to other living things rather than his distinctness from them. It is the fact that man alone was made "in the image of God" that makes him different from all other creatures: "So God created man in his own image, in the image of God he created him; male and female he created them. And God blessed them, and God said to them, 'Be fruitful and multiply, and fill the earth and subdue it; and have dominion over the fish of the sea and over the birds of the air and over every living thing that moves upon the earth'" (Gen. 1:27,28).

It seems that at least part of being made "in the image of God" involves man's responsibility for properly using the earth's resources. The results of sin can be clearly seen in what man has done with his "dominion." When we are fully conformed to Christ, then God's image will

111

be restored in us. Our intellect, emotions, will, plans, purpose and activities will be in complete harmony with God's will.

Language of Final Judgment and Destiny

When people ask, "Do you believe in a literal heaven and hell?" we are again confronted with the meaning of "literal." If the question is phrased "Do you believe in the reality of heaven and hell?" it takes on a different meaning.

The language describing heaven and hell are good examples of truth and reality being conveyed by "nonliteral" figures of speech: "Then I saw a great white throne and him who sat upon it; from his presence earth and sky fled away, and no place was found for them. And I saw the dead, great and small, standing before the throne, and books were opened. Also another book was opened, which is the book of life. And the dead were judged by what was written in the books, by what they had done. And the sea gave up the dead in it, Death and Hades gave up the dead in them, and all were judged by what they had done. Then Death and Hades were thrown into the lake of fire" (Rev. 20:11–14).

No one can read all of this passage with a strictly literal approach. The very terms Death and Hades are personified or they could not be "thrown into the lake of fire." Earth and sky are also personified for they "flee away."

There are anthropomorphisms in the description of God—i.e., He is described with the qualities of man. He is "seated upon a throne." Heaven and earth flee from his "face." Yet this figurative language is an effective way of conveying dramatic truths. God is a personal being, not an abstract force. He is a personal being of majesty and power.

The next sentence pictures the dead—the small and great—standing before the throne of God. The books are opened. This figure of speech is a bit archaic in modern times. A writer today would probably use the picture of electronic computers and tape recorders. Either way, the truth comes through that God knows the doings of men and the destiny of men. There is judgment after death and people will have to answer to God for what they are, what they have thought, and what they have done. Could this have been made so clear and forceful *except* through figurative language?

Death in the New Testament is called the last enemy to be abolished (see 1 Cor. 15:26,54,55). It is pictured as separation of a person from his body (see 2 Cor. 5:6–8; Phil. 1:21–24).

The Christian, though separated from his body, is in the presence of the Lord. Hades is pictured as the place of the dead and also as a place of punishment (see Luke 16:23). The non-Christian in Hades is separated from his body *and* from God. Physical death is the only separation that a Christian can experience, but for the one who rejects Jesus Christ, physical death is a prelude to total separation from God.

The reality of punishment leaps out through the figurative language in Revelation. The ultimate separation from God is described as the second death or the lake of fire. What dramatic language to show the wretchedness of being banished from the presence of God!

Understanding Language of Creation and Climax

1. Figurative language is the only possible way to convey realities that lie beyond human experience. Now we know only in part, but without such language, our ignorance would be total. Though our comprehension

may be small, it is extremely valuable. *It is all we need to know* to live richly and meaningfully with God and each other.

2. It is crucial that we understand the realities described by the language of creation and climax. We are deeply involved in the results of creation and will soon be active participants in the judgment, blessing or punishment of life after death.

3. We need to concentrate on the full impact of the truth this figurative language reveals. We tend to fill our lives with trivia and to delude ourselves into thinking that our present pattern of life is normal. Creation and climax speak to us about our *destiny*. They involve our relation to our Creator, our Redeemer and our Judge.

4. The truths of Scripture regarding creation and climax are not given to satisfy our scientific curiosity nor as a horoscope to the future. What we do not know must not become a battleground among Christians so that we lose sight of what we do know. The basic message of creation and climax is urgent and must be heard.

5. The kind of language employed ought to increase our awareness of how great God is. We must be careful not to diminish God to man-size.

Footnotes

1. Some of the material in this chapter is adapted from an unpublished paper entitled "Genesis One: A Working Approach," by Ronald Youngblood, professor of Old Testament Languages, Bethel Theological Seminary, St. Paul, Minnesota.
2. *Gesenius' Hebrew Grammar*, edited and enlarged by Kautzsch and Gowley, Oxford, 1910, paragraph 116a.

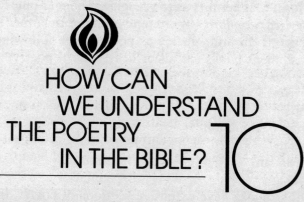

HOW CAN WE UNDERSTAND THE POETRY IN THE BIBLE?

10

For reasons that most of us cannot explain, poetry often seems to reach deeply into our souls. No careful analysis of the mechanics of poetry can tell us why some poems impress us so deeply.

C.S. Lewis observed that "only poetry can speak low enough to catch the faint murmur of the mind."[1]

Wordsworth said that poetry is "the overflow of spontaneous emotion recollected in tranquility."[2]

Poetry enlists the artist in the most blundering of us and for a few moments permits us to escape the cramped quarters of our own outlook. It opens our eyes, minds, and feelings to a rich world of reality to which most of us pay only fleeting visits.

Since poetry seems to reach into the very marrow of our bones, it is not surprising that much of the Bible is in poetry. This is especially true of the Old Testament, where Hebrews who felt deeply poured out their souls in poetry that still penetrates our beings many centuries later.

Those who use the *King James Version* or the *American Standard Version* of 1901 or *The Living Bible* may not be aware of how extensive poetry is in the Old Testament because the poetic sections are not printed in a form that permits us to recognize them as poetry. The *Revised Standard Version* and many of the other newer versions do print poetry as poetry. The following Old Testament books are all or nearly all in poetry:

Psalms	Lamentations
Proverbs	Amos
Job	Obadiah
Song of Solomon	Micah
Isaiah	Nahum
Jeremiah	Habakkuk
Joel	Zephaniah

Other books have extensive sections of poetry, including Ecclesiastes and Zechariah.

Read Poetry with a Poetic Frame of Mind

Regardless of how limited is our own poetic sense or our ability to produce poetry, we all know that we approach poetry with a different frame of mind than we use with prose. We come prepared with our imagination sharpened, our rhythmic senses ready to carry us along the swells and recesses. We are prepared for figures of speech, and we know better than to read poetry with a strictly literal approach. When we see something written in poetic form, our minds automatically prepare themselves to receive poetry.

This frame of mind is important as we study the poetic sections of the Old Testament. One of the tragedies of translations that do not print poetry as poetry is that the reader does not know when to make the mental and emotional transition to poetry.

Hebrew Poetic Form Is Different

Hebrew poetry is not like Western poetry. Much modern poetry and some ancient poetry is based on a balance of sound—phonetic rhythm. Nursery rhymes are a simple form of this balance of sound. Our more sophisticated poetry often does not incorporate rhyme at all, but it usually does have a certain balance of rhythm.

But Hebrew and Akkadian poetry (as well as Egyptian and Chinese) consist in a balance of thought rather than sound. It has a rhythm of *logic*. The poetry follows one idea by another line of thought parallel to the first. A verse consists of at least two parts in which the second part has a thought that is parallel to the first. This *parallelism* is the main feature of Hebrew poetry.

Although two lines usually constitute a verse, there are also three- four- and even five-line verses in Hebrew poetry. The balance of thought in these lines usually involves a certain number of stressed units in each line. In the most common two-line verses, there are often three stressed units in each line. Look at Psalm 103:10 (literal translation):

Not-according-to-our-sins / did-he-act / toward-us
Not-according-to-our-iniquities / did he deal fully / against us.

This parallelism in which the second line repeats the same ideas as the first is the most common type and is known as *synonymous parallelism*.

The poetic Hebrews did not limit themselves to one form. They also used *contrasting parallelism*, in which the second line expresses a thought in sharp contrast to that of the first line. Proverbs 15:1 is an example (literal translation):

A-gentle-answer / turns-away / rage
But-word-that-hurts / stirs-up / anger.

There is also *parallelism of emblems*. In this form, one line uses a figurative statement and the other line a more literal one, as in Psalm 42:1 (literal translation):

As-a-hart / longs / for-flowing-streams

117

So-my-soul / longs / for-thee-O-God.

Another fascinating variation in Hebrew poetry is *stair-like parallelism*. In this form a part of the first line is repeated while newer elements build up to a climax. This is seen in Psalm 29:1,2 *(RSV)*.

Ascribe / to-the-Lord / O-heavenly-beings
Ascribe / to-the-Lord / glory-and-strength
Ascribe / to-the-Lord / the-glory-of-his-name.

The Hebrew poets were not slaves to any form. We often find their parallelism incomplete, with some units missing. This is their kind of "free verse." In the illustration just given, the third unit of the first line is not really parallel to the third unit of the second and third lines. Sometimes incomplete parallelism is compensated for by adding other stressed units that are not parallel in thought, as in Psalm 103:15 (literal translation):

As-for-man / his-days / are-as-the-green-grass
As-the-flowers-of-the-field / so / he-blossoms.

Whether the parallelism is complete or not, the reader who knows he is reading poetry is carried along as the prophets pour forth their anguish, their joys, their expectations from God, their concerns for themselves and their people.

Stanzas in Hebrew Poetry

For the past one hundred years, there has been prolonged discussion and some disagreement among scholars as to how Hebrew poetry is grouped to form stanzas. There are differences of opinion where the author has not clearly indicated his intention by some Hebrew device. There were two devices which, when used, made the intention of the author clear.

Sometimes the Hebrews used a *recurring refrain* to indicate the opening or closing of a stanza. In Psalm 136, the words "for his steadfast love endures for ever" recurs after every line. However, this demands an intolerable number of stanzas, so editors have grouped the ideas together to form longer stanzas. Sometimes ideas are clearly grouped, and this kind of stanza division then becomes easy.

Some Hebrew poets gave a sure indication of stanzas by use of *an acrostic.* In this device, a group of lines begins with the first letter of the Hebrew alphabet, followed by the next letter for the next group. This accounts for the length of Psalm 119 where the author used eight consecutive lines beginning with the first letter of the Hebrew alphabet, followed by eight lines beginning with the second letter, eight lines with the third, and so on through the twenty-two letters of the Hebrew alphabet.

Other acrostic poems are found in Psalms 25,35 and 145, where each two-line verse begins with consecutive letters of the Hebrew alphabet. The beautiful Lamentations chapters 1,2,3,4 are based on a similar acrostic. Although the acrostic idea seems artificial and self-limiting to us, the Hebrew poets were apparently able to rise above such limitations, for few passages are more picturesque than Lamentations 1—4.

The majority of Hebrew poetry does not have such clear indications of stanzas, however, and in these cases the poetic paragraphing (stanzas) of the translators must guide us. Unless we pay attention to these smaller units we will not be able to understand the whole.

Poetry Is Personal

Poetry is essentially a personal experience—both to the writer and to the reader. We dare not become absorbed in the mechanics of it. We should concentrate rather on the personal quality of the poetry, especially in the Psalms, for this is what attracts so many day after day. The reader can enter into the rich experiences of the poet and there find that the language of the poet expresses his own longings, hopes, disappointments and trials.

Most readers would find it a worthy experience to read through the book of Lamentations at a single sitting. The poet has shared the calamity of his own people and he expresses not only his own sorrows and sufferings but the collective sorrow and suffering of his people. Out of deep pessimism he also recounts their only hope in Lamentations 3:22,23 (literal translation):

It is the steadfast hope of Jehovah,
> that we do not come to an end;
> that his mercies do not fail.
> They are new every morning.

Great is Thy faithfulness.

The poet finds that he can face reality because he stands face to face with God.

Poetry Is Rich in Imagery

By its very nature, poetry lends itself to figurative language. The Hebrews were masters of figurative language even in prose, and in poetry their intense creativity in figurative language had full reign. The passage in Isaiah 1:2,3 illustrates this:

"Hear, O heavens, and give ear, O earth;
> for the Lord has spoken:
'Sons have I reared and brought up,
> but they have rebelled against me.
The ox knows its owner,
> and the ass its master's crib;
but Israel does not know,
> my people do not understand.' "

Here a personified heaven and earth are asked to listen to the charge of the Lord. The sons whom he has

120

reared have rebelled against him. The ox and ass know their master, but not so God's people. The passage (vv. 5,6) goes on to describe Israel as one in whom

"The whole head is sick,
   and the whole heart faint.
From the sole of the foot even to the head,
   there is no soundness in it,
but bruises and sores
   and bleeding wounds;
they are not pressed out, or bound up,
    or softened with oil."

The nation of Israel is personified as a sick and bruised person.

The entire chapter is rich in imagery, all taken from the daily life of the people. Most of it is taken from their agrarian economy, and although we no longer live in this kind of society, the imagery still speaks strongly to us.

Understanding Poetry in Psalms

1. If possible, try to find the historical occasion for the particular psalm. The content of the psalm and the individual psalm title often give clues. A good commentary may help. However, it is better to admit ignorance of the particular context than to assign it arbitrarily to a particular historical occasion if there is not enough evidence to justify such as assignment.

2. Try to understand the attitude, the outlook, the spiritual and psychological mood of the poet when he composed the psalm. Calvin called the Psalms, "an anatomy of all parts of the soul."[3]

3. In dealing with the imprecatory psalms (those in which the psalmist hurls curses at his enemies) such as Psalm 109:6–20 and Psalm 137:7–9, regard such passages as poetic expressions of persons who were in-

censed at the tyranny of evil. They are so colored by their sense of being wronged or by their outrage at the blasphemy committed that they forget to leave judgment to God. These psalms show what injustice and evil can do even to a good man. For further discussion see C.S. Lewis, *Reflections on the Psalms.*[4]

4. In the messianic psalms (2,16,22,40,45,69,72,98, 110 and others) note the elements that applied to the time of the writer as well as to the time of Christ. Consider why certain factors, because of what they involve, could only belong in the highest degree to the Messiah. The beauty of expression in these psalms must be appreciated in terms of the historical perspective at the time of their writing.

5. Observe the poet's basic convictions about God. The poet returns to these convictions when he feels the mounting pressures of life.

Understanding Poetry in Proverbs

1. Proverbs is a group of maxims or short sagacious sayings that were taken from everyday life and handed down from one generation to another. The fact that these sayings were handed down in poetic form is another indication of the artistic temperament of the Hebrew people.

2. The proverbs deal with problems of personal life, of interpersonal relationships, of our relationship with God, of moral principles, of attitude toward possessions, and other topics.

3. Unlike us, the Hebrews made no distinction between what is secular and what is sacred. They believed that God was the God of the whole earth who exercised authority in every aspect of life.

4. Although we may classify the proverbs as to subject matter, we should not think of some as "religious"

and others as "nonreligious." This is foreign to the thinking of the Hebrew people from whom these proverbs come.

5. Some proverbs are obscure. Occasionally the context may shed some light on the meaning because some proverbs are grouped together so that a common or parallel theme is developed. If the obscurity cannot be removed, admit it freely and center attention on the sections that *can* be understood. Watch for short figures of speech in Proverbs and apply the principles discussed in chapter 7.

Job—the Greatest Old Testament Poetry

The prologue and epilogue of Job are in prose. The remainder of the book is in poetry. The prologue (Job 1:1—2:13) gives the setting of the book—the faithfulness of Job, the council in the court of heaven, the misfortunes of Job, and the visit of his three friends. The epilogue (Job 42:7–17) describes the restoration of Job.

The remaining 40 chapters of Job are written in poetry. The poet wrestles with the basic question of mankind: What is the meaning of life? This question finds no easy answer in Job. There are related questions: How does the man of faith react to suffering? How can a person approach God? What is the meaning of faith, of integrity, of purpose? These all point us to the reality of God, even though we do not have the answers for life's enigmas.

Job is probably the greatest poetry in the Old Testament. The writer is eloquent, versatile, vigorous, and concise. To get the most out of studying Job, observe the following suggestions:

1. Study the complete utterances of the main characters: Job, Eliphaz, Bildad, Zophar, and Elihu. Find out what are the basic assumptions of each one, and evalu-

ate their arguments with these in mind.

2. Study the declarations of God. See why there is such a stress on Job's ignorance, and how this is related to the self-confidence of the other characters.

3. Recognize the basic questions and the answers that are given to them. We are tempted to look for answers to questions that the author did not discuss and then we are annoyed by his lack of answers to our chosen questions! Be aware that only certain aspects of questions are discussed. On these particular aspects there is a good deal of illumination. This illumination is of the searchlight variety, however, with many facets of the topic still in the dark. Job himself had to find out that it was not information he needed so much as he needed God Himself, "I had heard of thee by the hearing of the ear; but now mine eye seeth thee" (Job 42:5, *KJV*).

Understanding Poetry in the Prophets

1. Try to see the prophet as a person and as a poet.

2. Use the standard sound procedures of studying context, history and culture to see the specific situation out of which the poetry arose.

3. Note how the poetic imagery and the personal dimension of the prophet speak to us, enabling us to enter into his situation and to share his message from God.

Footnotes

1. C.S. Lewis, *Letters to Malcolm.* (New York: Harcourt Brace Jovanovich, Inc., 1963), p. 112.
2. William Wordsworth, *Lyrical Ballads.* 2nd ed. (New York: Oxford University Press, 1969), Preface.
3. John Calvin, *Commentary on the Book of Psalms* (1845), I, xxxxvi.
4. C.S. Lewis, "The Cursings," *Reflections on the Psalms.* (New York: *Harcourt Brace Jovanovich, Inc., 1958), pp. 20–33.*

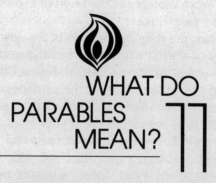

WHAT DO
PARABLES
MEAN? 11

One of the main vehicles of Jesus' teaching is the parable. From the early Church fathers through the Middle Ages the parables of Jesus have probably suffered as much abuse in interpretation as any section of the Bible. The reason for this is that interpreters have attempted to allegorize them.

Allegorizing means that a text may be interpreted apart from its grammatical and historical meaning, so that what the original writer meant can be largely ignored. Every little point of a story can be given some meaning that is chosen largely at the discretion (or indiscretion!) of the interpreter. (For further information about allegorizing read chapter 12).

Parables were not intended to be allegorized. Jesus used parables to throw light on the reign of God and on the response of people to the demands of God. The parables should be read in the light of the primary thrust of Jesus' message—the breaking in of the reign of God.

The Hearers of the Parable

Some who heard Jesus teach were amazed because He "taught them as one who had authority, and not as their scribes" (Matt. 7:29). Not only did Jesus reveal authority in how He *taught* but also in what He *did*. His miracles were samples of the reign of God that He came to declare (see Luke 11:20).

However, the religious leaders of the Jews resisted the authority of Christ's teaching and the authority of His acts. They sent officers to arrest Jesus. The officers returned to the leaders without their prisoner but with the explanation, "No man ever spoke like this man" (John 7:46). The priests and Pharisees angrily insisted that the crowd didn't know the Law as they did and that the crowd was accursed (see John 7:47–49). The religious leaders explained away Jesus' miracles by saying that Jesus was in league with Beelzebub, the prince of demons (see Luke 11:15; Matt. 12:24).

For people with this mind-set, parables would teach nothing. And for those under the influence of the Pharisees, the parables would appear as obscure riddles.

The parable of the different kinds of soil and its explanation is recorded in Matthew 13:1–23; Mark 4:1–20, and Luke 8:4–15. In all three accounts, between the parable and the explanation, is a small section on the reason Jesus used parables.

Jesus knew that, although the crowds trailed after Him, most of them did not actually understand His good news about the reign of God. Both the "insiders" (the disciples and others who faithfully followed Jesus) and the "outsiders" (who were spectators but not followers in heart) heard the parables. Both groups saw what Jesus did and heard Him answer questions put to Him in public. One group responded and believed; the other group did not.

The explanation in the parable of the sower discusses Jesus' use of the parable as representative of all Jesus' teaching. Why did some respond in faith and others not?

One reason is the *action of God:* "To you it has been given to know the secrets of the kingdom of God; but for others they are in parables, so that seeing they may not see, and hearing they may not understand" (Luke 8:9,10; see also Mark 4:10–12).

The second reason is the *attitude of men* themselves as seen in Matthew 13:13–16: "This is why I speak to them in parables, because seeing they do not see, and hearing they do not hear, nor do they understand. With them indeed is fulfilled the prophecy of Isaiah which says:

"'You shall indeed hear but never understand,
and you shall indeed see but never perceive.
For this people's heart has grown dull,
and their ears are heavy of hearing,
and their eyes they have closed,
lest they should perceive with their eyes,
and hear with their ears,
and understand with their heart,
and turn for me to heal them.' "

Apparently both God's sovereignty and people's responses influence their understanding of the parables. Although parables are a powerful kind of teaching, the very nature of what Jesus had to say and the spiritual condition of His listeners made some parables obscure.

The Setting for the Parable
The setting of the incident or teaching is important in

nearly all Bible study. However, Jesus often told His parables more than once. For example, the parable of the lost sheep is found twice in the Gospels to teach two different lessons.

In Luke 15:1–7, Jesus told the parable of the lost sheep to the Pharisees and scribes who were complaining because Jesus associated with "sinners." The story involved the man with 100 sheep who lost one, left the 99, and searched until he found the missing sheep. He brought it home on his shoulder, rejoicing all the way. When he arrived, he invited his friends and neighbors to rejoice with him because he had found the lost sheep.

Jesus stressed the point of joy over the recovery of the lost. Christ was telling His critics: "I associate with sinners because their response to me will bring a change of mind on their part and forgiveness of sins. God rejoices over those who come back to Him." In this instance the setting for the parable, the audience, was Jesus' critics.

The same parable is recorded in Matthew 18:12–14. But this time Jesus spoke only to the disciples. He set a child in the midst of the group and said, "Whoever humbles himself like this child, he is the greatest in the kingdom of heaven" (Matt. 18:4). Christ then discussed the influence of adults on children, "Whoever causes one of these little ones who believe in me to sin" would be better off dead (Matt. 18:6). He told the disciples that they must be concerned about the welfare of little children, and at this point He told the parable of the lost sheep and closed it with, "So it is not the will of my Father who is in heaven that one of these little ones should perish" (v. 14).

Thus Jesus used the same parable to teach two lessons. In Luke the lesson is that God has compassion toward sinners. In Matthew, it is that God has concern for believers—in this case children.

A Conclusion to the Parable

At the close of some of the parables, there is a terse teaching that sums up the lesson. Sometimes the same conclusion is attached to several different parables. Jesus apparently used story after story to drive home certain important principles.

For example, in Matthew 20:1-16, we read the parable about the workers in the vineyard who were hired at different times of the day, but at the end of the day all were paid for a full day's work. Those who had worked the full day complained to the owner that they should have received some special bonus since they had worked longer than the others. The owner answered, "Do you begrudge my generosity toward those who were not able to find work at the beginning of the day?" Then Jesus concludes with, "So the last will be first, and the first last" (v. 16). The conclusion emphasizes the goodness of the owner in paying them all enough to support themselves and their families.

The same conclusion followed Jesus' interview with the rich young ruler and His comment about how hard it is for the rich to enter the Kindgom of God (see Matt. 19:16-30). Peter replied that the disciples had left everything to follow Jesus. Jesus then said: "Every one who has left houses or brothers or sisters or father or mother or children or lands, for my name's sake, will receive a hundredfold and inherit eternal life. But many that are first will be last, and the last first" (vv. 29,30).

In the parable of the vineyard, the emphasis is on the last being first. In the section on leaving houses and lands, the stress is on the first being last.

The same saying is repeated in a still different setting. Jesus had just explained that the way to the Kingdom of God is narrow and that many who claim to be followers will be turned away. They will weep and gnash their teeth when they see Abraham, Isaac, Jacob, and the prophets in the Kingdom, and themselves thrust out (see Luke 13:22–29). Then comes the line, "And behold, some are last who will be first, and some are first who will be last" (v. 30).

Sometimes the generalizing conclusion at the end of a parable referred to only one small aspect of the parable, and sometimes to the main thrust. Furthermore, the application of the parable was sometimes a theme that entered into many aspects of Jesus' teaching.

For example, in the parable of the talents in Matthew 25:14–30, Jesus tells of a man who, about to leave for a journey, called in his slaves and gave each of them some money to invest. To one he gave five talents, to another two talents, and to the third, one talent. (Each talent is estimated as worth about a thousand dollars.) Later, the master returned to see how well each of his slaves had invested his money. The one who had received five talents had used it to earn five talents more; the one with two talents had also doubled his investment. The one who had received one talent simply returned it to his owner with the excuse that he was afraid of his master. The master rebuked him for failing to invest his money and commanded that it be taken from him and given to the most productive slave. Then the saying is recorded, "For to every one who has will more be given, and he will have abundance; but from him who has not, even what he has will be taken away" (Matt. 25:29).

This saying also appears in Matthew 13:12, Mark 4:25 and Luke 8:18. In Matthew 13 and Mark 4 Jesus includes a warning that His hearers should be alert to what they hear. The context indicates that the real meaning of "hearing" in this case is "obeying." A close study of all these sections indicates that Jesus was stressing the difference between the person who is static and the one who is growing in obedience to God and in the knowledge of God. Unless we grow spiritually, "even what we have" will be taken from us. As we grow in obedience and knowledge, our capacity to grow increases and "more is given to us." This is obviously an important truth since it is repeated many times in the teachings of Jesus.

Sometimes what appears to be a conclusion to a parable or to two parables is actually the conclusion to a section in which certain parables are used to enforce the main teaching.

For example, two parables appear in Luke 14:25–35 where Jesus taught the importance of considering the cost of discipleship. He begins, in verse 26, "If any one comes to me and does not hate his own father and mother and wife and children and brothers and sisters, yes, and even his own life, he cannot be my disciple." ("Hate" in this case is obviously hyperbole—conscious overstatement.) Then come the two parables. The first is about a man who builds a tower and who must know the exact cost before he starts or he will be embarrassed by not being able to finish it. The second discusses the importance of a king assessing his strength before he goes to war.

Then comes the conclusion, "So therefore, whoever of you does not renounce all that he has cannot be my disciple." This conclusion is not actually that of either parable, but of the total teaching that personal loyalties cannot come before loyalty to Christ and that discipleship involves counting the cost.

The Primary Focus of the Parable

The parables cannot be studied apart from the total teachings of Christ. Because parables usually focus on one main point of comparison, this chief point must be related to the central idea in Jesus' message.

The reign of God was the center of Jesus' message. The Greek word *basileia*, which designates the royal reign or Kingdom of God, appears more than a hundred times in the Gospels. The parables illustrated and unfolded various aspects of the reign of God.

In the parable of the tares (weeds) and the wheat (see Matt. 13:24–30), Jesus showed that the reign of God is here now but it is not absolute. The weeds are not uprooted now because the process may damage the wheat, "Let both grow together until the harvest" (Matt. 13:30), then the weeds will be burned and the wheat stored in the barn.

Later, at the insistence of the disciples, Jesus explained the parable. In the explanation, He treated it as an allegory. (Using an allegory as a way of teaching is not the same as "allegorizing" a parable). The sower is the Son of man; the field is the world. The good seed refers to the sons of the Kingdom, and the weeds are the sons of the evil one. The one who sowed the weeds is the devil. The harvest is the close of the age; the reapers are angels.

Then Jesus gave a brief description of the consummation of history when the reign of God will be total: "The Son of man will send his angels, and they will gather out of his kingdom all causes of sin and all evildoers, and throw them into the furnace of fire; there men will weep and gnash their teeth. Then the righteous will shine like the sun in the kingdom of their Father" (Matt. 13:36–43). This is all in the *future* tense, when the reign of God is complete.

Jesus underscored the *present* aspect of the reign of God in His parable about the difficulty of plundering a strong man's house unless the robber first binds the strong man. The Pharisees had accused Jesus of working

His miracles by the power of Beelzebub, the prince of demons (see Matt. 12:24; Mark 3:22). Jesus replied with a series of short parables about a divided kingdom, a divided city, and divided house that cannot stand. Satan does not cast out Satan (see Matt. 12:25–29).

The parables of the strong man's house being plundered focused on Jesus' miraculous deeds as proof of His power to bind Satan, "If it is by the Spirit of God that I cast out demons, then the kingdom of God has come upon you" (Matt. 12:28).

The miracles of Jesus were samples of Christ's power and what the reign of God will be like when it comes in its fullness.

In Matthew 21:28–32, Jesus told the religious leaders (Pharisees, chief priests, scribes) the parable of the two sons who were asked by their father to work in the vineyard. The first son refused but later repented and did go and work. The second son said he would, but did not do so. Then Jesus asked, "Which of the two did the will of his father?" (v. 31). They answered, "The first."

Jesus applied the parable by saying that the harlots and tax collectors were represented by the first son, and the religious leaders were represented by the second. Grace provided both sons the opportunity of showing their willingness to obey their father. What made the difference was their response.

In the parable of the lost sheep in Luke 15:1–7, the role of God's grace is seen when the shepherd takes the initiative to look for the lost sheep until he finds it. God rejoices at the response to His grace.

Two parables apply to great crises in the reign of God.

The first parable is that of the wicked tenants of the vineyard who killed the owner's son (see Matt. 21:33–46; Mark 12:1–12; Luke 20:9–19). A man planted a vineyard, equipped it well, and leased it out to tenants to operate on a share basis. At the time of harvest, he sent his servants to collect his share of the harvest. They were refused and abused. Some were beaten, some stoned, some killed. He sent more representatives who received the same treatment. Finally he sent his son, feeling sure they would respect him. But the tenants killed him, thinking they could thereby get his inheritance. Christ then asked, what will the owner do? He will destroy those tenants and give the vineyard to others.

Matthew 21:43 records Jesus' application: "Therefore I tell you, the kingdom of God will be taken away from you and given to a nation producing the fruits of it."

All three accounts say that the Jewish leaders recognized that the parable was addressed to them and their anger was so great that they wanted to arrest Jesus immediately, but they were afraid of the crowd. The "nation producing the fruits of it" is identified as the Christian Church in 1 Peter 2:9,10. This parable of crisis referred to Jesus' earthly life and death.

Another parable referred to a crisis yet to come—the return of Christ to complete His messianic work. This is the parable of the ten bridesmaids (or virgins)—five foolish and five wise (Matt. 25:1–13). The wise virgins were prepared at all times for the coming of the bridegroom; the foolish ones ran out of oil for their lamps. Jesus concluded with, "Watch therefore, for you know neither the day nor the hour" (v. 13).

Interpreting Jesus' Parables

1. Seek to understand the earthly details of the parables.

2. Note the attitudes and spiritual condition of the original hearers.

3. Try to find what prompted Jesus to tell the parable.

Often parables were one of Jesus' methods of presenting fresh truths to people who were opposed to His innovations, or who needed instructions as to what the reign of God really involved.

4. Be sure you understand the focus—the *main point of the parable.*

5. Try to relate the main point of the parable to the basic teaching of Jesus—the centrality of the reign of God.

6. Look for any generalized saying in the parable. Such a saying may be the central point of the parable, or only a side point.

7. See how the main point may be related to people in our day, living in situations very different from those in the original setting.

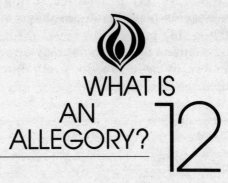

WHAT IS AN ALLEGORY? 12

Whereas Jesus used parables very often, He used only a few allegories. A parable, roughly defined, is an extended simlie, and an allegory is a longer metaphor. Parables and allegories have many differences, as the following chart shows:

In a parable:	In an allegory:
1. Words are used *literally*.	1. Words are used *figuratively*.
2. There is *one* chief point of comparison.	2. There are *several* points of comparison.
3. Imagery is kept *distinct* from the thing it signifies.	3. Imagery is *identified* with the things it signifies.
4. The meaning is explained by telling	4. The meaning is explained by showing

what the imagery stands for in light of the main point of the story.	*why* the imagery is identified with reality and what specific truths are taught.
5. The story is *true to the facts and experiences of life.*	5. The story blends *factual experience with non-factual* experience to enable the narrative to teach specific truths.

An Allegory Uses Words Figuratively

An allegory is a story or teaching that is meant to convey a figurative meaning. Nearly every main factor in the story or teaching stands for something specific.

In the familiar allegory of the Good Shepherd in John 10:1–16, Jesus said that He represented the door of the sheepfold; that He also represented the good shepherd; that the sheep were those for whom Christ laid down His life, and the flock represented the union of all believers regardless of their cultural or national heritage (John 10:7–16).

Difficulties with allegories arise when the interpreter insists that *every* point has to convey some specific comparison. For example, do we identify the hireling who fled (John 10:12) with the religious leaders of the day, or was it simply a part of the story inserted to bring out the true concern of the shepherd? It is not necessary to compare every point.

Allegories Are in Both Testaments

True allegories appear both in the Old and New Testaments. Their explanations usually accompany them, but not always. In Psalm 80:8–18, Israel is portrayed as a vine brought out of Egypt. Although no explanation accompanies it, the meaning is clear to the reader.

In Proverbs 5:15–19, marital fidelity is extolled by urging that a man drink from his own cistern and no one else's. The explanation follows in verses 20–23 where the commandment is repeated in plain non-allegorical language.

A brilliant allegory appears in Ecclesiastes 12:3–7, where old age is depicted as a household that is ceasing to function.

In Ezekiel 13:8–16, false prophets are described unforgettably as men who build a wall and try to hold it together with whitewash.

In the New Testament there are many important allegories. One is of the vine and the branches (John 15:1–10), and another is Paul's allegory of the building (1 Cor. 3:10–15). There is also the description of the Christian's armor as weapons of offense and defense in Ephesians 6:10–17, and that of Christ as the Good Shepherd in John 10:1–16.

Perhaps the most famous allegory is that of the Last Supper, which also included dramatization, in Matthew 26:26–29, Mark 14:22–25, and Luke 22:14–23. Jesus took bread and broke it, saying, "Take, eat; this is my body." Then He took the cup and said, "Drink of it, all of you; for this is my blood of the covenant, which is poured out for many for the forgiveness of sins" (Matt. 26:26–28).

The fact that this is allegory does not make its truth any less real. The allegory had two parts and Jesus named them clearly—the bread, which is His body; and the wine, His blood, which is poured out for many for the forgiveness of sins.

Allegories Emphasize Something Important

The story of the vine and the branches (John 15:1–10) shows how Christ used allegory to teach something important. Jesus made three main comparisons.

The first comparison stresses the importance of the vine (Christ) and its relationship to the branches (believers). "Apart from me you [plural] can do nothing" (John 15:5).

The second comparison emphasizes the action of the vinedresser, the Father (John 15:1). If a branch does not bear fruit, the vinedresser cuts it off. The branches that do bear fruit he prunes so that they will bear more fruit. The Father is concerned about fruit bearing. He takes drastic action to eliminate fruitless branches and to bring to maximum production the branches attached to the vine.

The last major comparison is that of branches to believers (John 15:5). This illustrates one of the frequent characteristics of allegory—the blending of factual experience with non-factual experience so that the narrative can teach specific truths. In the allegory of the vine and the branches, the branches "abide" in the vine. Actually, a branch cannot choose to "abide" in the vine. It cannot choose to do anything. Yet in the allegory, the disciples are commanded to "abide in me" as an obvious act of the will. Verse 6 reads, "If a man does not abide in me, he is cast forth as a branch and withers; and the branches are gathered, thrown into the fire and burned."

Obviously Jesus was not thinking of the inanimate connection of a branch to the vine. He was thinking of an active, vital relationship, for verse 7 reads, "If you abide in me, and my words abide in you, ask whatever you will, and it shall be done for you." Jesus was saying that answers to prayer depend on this active relationship.

Fruit-bearing, in verse 8, is said to be proof of discipleship and a means of glorifying God. Obeying Christ's commandments shows that the disciple is abiding in

Christ's love (15:9,10). The allegory dynamically portrays why the believer must maintain a fresh, vital relationship with Christ.

Allegory and Allegorizing

Allegory as used by Jesus is a legitimate way of teaching truth and should not be confused with allegorizing. In allegorizing, a simple *historical* narrative or parable is made to teach something entirely different from that intended by the original writer. The interpreter ignores what the original writer meant and looks for hidden "spiritual" meanings.

There is only one clear example of allegorizing in the New Testament. That example is in Galatians 4:21–31, and Paul clearly labels it. Paul allegorizes by saying that two women, Hagar and Sarah, represent the two covenants. Hagar represents the Old Covenant (Judaism) and Mount Sinai; Sarah represents the New Covenant, the New Jerusalem.

Allegorizing was prominent in Greek thought at least 500 years before the time of Christ. The fact that allegorizing is so rare in the New Testament is significant. It came into Jewish thought via the Greeks and there is evidence that the Jews allegorized the Old Testament as early as 200 B.C.

A famous letter of Aristeas (an Alexandrian Jew), written about 100 B.C., allegorizes the dietary laws of the Old Testament to say that they really taught various kinds of discrimination to obtain virtue. For example, animals chewing or not chewing the cud "is nothing else than the reminiscence of life and existence."[1]

Philo, an Alexandrian Jewish philosopher who lived about the time of Christ, made allegorizing his principle method of interpreting the Old Testament.

Allegorizing was common in the Church from the time

of Origen (A.D. 200) until nearly the time of Luther (A.D. 1500). Examples for this period show that this kind of interpretation was more concerned with what the interpreter wanted to say than with what the Bible actually taught.

Although Origen was an excellent scholar and had an outstanding knowledge of the Bible, he was influenced by the thinking of his time and developed some fanciful interpretations. To Origen, Rebekah's drawing water for Abraham's servant (Gen. 24:15–21) meant that we must come to the wells of Scripture to meet Christ.

Origen interpreted the story of the triumphal entry of Christ thus: The ass represents the letter of the Old Testament; the colt or foal of the ass speaks of the New Testament; the two apostles who obtained the animals and brought them to Jesus are the moral and spiritual senses.

One preacher in the fifth century allegorized on Herod's slaughter of the infants at Bethlehem this way: the fact that only the children two years old and under were murdered while those of three presumably escaped is meant to teach us that those who hold the Trinitarian faith will be saved, whereas Binitarians and Unitarians will undoubtedly perish.[2]

Such allegorizing tells the listener or reader what the *interpreter* is thinking but tells nothing about what the *biblical writer* was saying. His meaning is ignored.

Even Augustine, saint and scholar that he was, allegorized extensively. For example, in Psalm 3:5, the psalmist talks of lying down, sleeping, and rising or awakening. Augustine says that the psalmist is really referring to the death and resurrection of Christ.

During the Middle Ages there came into prominence the "fourfold interpretation" idea. This was expressed poetically:

141

"The letter shows us what God and our fa-
thers did;
The allegory shows us where our faith is hid;
The moral meaning gives us rules of daily life;
The anagogy shows us where to end our
strife."

("Anagogy" refers to the Christian's future hope.)

To medieval interpreters, the literal meaning of Jerusalem was the city in Palestine. Allegorically it meant the Church. Morally it referred to the human soul. Anagogically, Jerusalem referred to the heavenly city.

Although allegorizing and the "fourfold method" were diminishing slightly by the time of Martin Luther, his lectures on Romans and on the Psalms, plus his own independent study of Scripture, made him discontented with the traditionalism and allegorizing of the Church of Rome. This dissatisfaction helped prepare him for positive action. Later he abandoned completely the fourfold interpretation of the medieval period and stressed the single fundamental meaning.

Allegorizing Removes Certainty of Meaning

The pursuit of multiple meanings is really a magical approach to language that removes any certainty of meaning. It is true that one passage of Scripture may incorporate teachings about a man's conduct, belief, and hope, but not all of these ideas are expressed by the original writer in the same word or phrase.

One particular expression like "Jerusalem" *in any one passage has only one meaning.* Where it means the literal earthly city, it does not refer to the heavenly city. In each context the train of thought must determine the meaning in that place.

Allegorizing makes it impossible to handle objectively

either literal or figurative language. It is like a fog that first renders objects indistinct and finally blots them out altogether.

Understanding Allegories

1. With allegory, as with other portions of the Bible, it is important to know who were the original hearers.

2. Try to understand why the speaker or writer used the allegory in the first place.

3. Look for the basic points of comparison stressed by the original speaker or writer. Look for explicit identification such as, "I am the true vine, and my Father is the vinedresser," in John 15:1. If there is no explicit identification, look for meaning given in the context.

4. State simply why these truths were essential for the original hearer or reader and why they are essential for us today.

Footnotes

1. R.H. Charles, et al, ed., "Letter of Aristeas, 154," (See 150–156.), *Apocrypha and Pseudepigrapha of the Old Testament*, Vol. 2, (New York: Oxford University Press, 1913), pp. 108, 109.
2. G.W.H. Lempe and K.J. Woolcombe, *Essays on Typology*, Studies in Biblical Theology series. (London: SCM Press, 1957), pp. 30, 31.

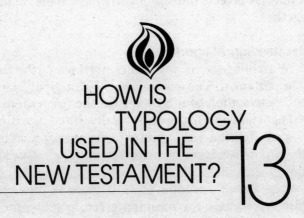

HOW IS TYPOLOGY USED IN THE NEW TESTAMENT? 13

Typology is used extensively in the New Testament. Typology is a correspondence of one or, at the most, two points between a person, event or thing in the Old Testament and a person, event or thing in the New Testament. Typology should not be confused with allegorizing. In typology the things compared are *always actual historical events, persons or things.*

The correspondence is present because God controls history. This understanding of God's control over history is basic to the New Testament writers: God caused earlier individuals, groups, experiences, etc., to embody characteristics that later He would cause to reappear.

For example, the experience of the children of Israel being bitten by serpents in the desert is handled typologically in the New Testament. The Old Testament account in Numbers 21:6–9 tells that fiery serpents were sent among the people. The serpents bit the people and caused many of them to die. Moses made a bronze serpent and set it on a pole. Everyone bitten by a serpent who looked at the model recovered.

In John 3:14, this Old Testament event is said to be

a "type" of the New Testament event of Christ's death upon a cross: "And as Moses lifted up the serpent in the wilderness, so must the Son of man be lifted up, that whoever believes in him may have eternal life."

Points of correspondence are: (1) the lifting up of the serpent and of Christ, and (2) life for those who respond to the object lifted up. In both points the typology makes a higher application of meaning than the original. Both the serpent and Christ were literally lifted up. Both events occurred in history. But the meaning of the "lifting up" of Christ in crucifixion is infinitely greater. The same is true of the response. Those who looked at the bronze serpent "lived" in the sense that they did not then die of snakebite. Those who commit themselves to Christ have "eternal life," a new quality of life both in the now and in the life to come.

Before we can understand typology, we must recognize a very important concept: *God speaks through His people.* To the writers of the Bible, God is not an abstraction. He is a God who acts, who reveals Himself, who is known by His people, through His people, and among His people. This relationship with His people opens fellowship with God Himself. Thus the people of God are the divinely chosen means through which other people acquire a fully developed knowledge of God.

Israel was the people of God in the Old Testament. In the New Testament, God brought into being a new people of God not restricted by national origins. Many people have been blended into one new people through God's act in sending Christ and through faith or commitment of persons to Christ. (See Titus 2:14; Heb. 13: 12; 1 Pet. 2:9,10; Rev. 21:3.)

The people of God are one because they receive God's promises and experience their fulfillment. This is the "messianic community," including all people of

God, whether part of the Old Covenant with Israel, or the New Covenant under Christ.

Being bound to Christ, the messianic community of the New Testament times saw all of the shadowy representations of the Old Testament replaced by direct access to God, by a final sacrifice, and by demonstrations or proof of the Spirit and of power (see 1 Cor. 2:4,5).

During some periods of history there has been an exaggerated emphasis on typology. Because of such extremes, the pendulum swung so far the other way that any study of "types" was looked upon with suspicion. Both extremes prevent understanding. History indicates that it is difficult to maintain a balance in typology, but a biblical emphasis on God and His people in history helps us to use typology in a worthy manner.

What Makes a True Type?

Three factors are important in determining a true "type." *First*, some notable point of resemblance must exist between the type (earlier occurrence) and its antitype (the thing that occurred later).

Second, even though a person, event, or thing in the Old Testament may be a true type, it does not mean that the original people involved recognized it as typical. For example, the wilderness generation knew only that the bronze serpent saved them from dying of snakebite. They had no concept of the typological meaning that would appear in the New Testament.

Third, the point of correspondence is important for later people (those of the time of the antitype) because they can see that God's earlier action became more significant by His later action.

"Types" of Christ

New Testament writers have used specific characteristics or relationships of Solomon, David, Isaiah and Melchizedek and applied them typologically to Christ.

In John 2:13–17, Jesus cleanses the Temple, driving out the money-changers and overturning their tables. John records, "His disciples remembered that it was written, 'Zeal for thy house will consume me' " (v. 17).

Those words are from Psalm 69:9 which reads, "For zeal for thy house has consumed me, and the insults of those who insult thee have fallen on me." In its original setting, it was the cry of the psalm writer in deep distress over his many enemies and foes. He felt that he would be overwhelmed. His wrongdoings were not hidden from God. But he pleaded for God to act. He insisted that he had been reproached and borne shame on behalf of God. In a very limited way, his experiences were said to be a type of Christ's experiences. The point of comparison is that both Jesus and the psalmist had a zeal for the place where God was worshiped.

The second portion of Psalm 69:9 was used in another typological way in Romans 15:3. In this chapter, Paul told Christians that they must be concerned about the welfare of each other and not just of themselves, "For Christ did not please himself; but, as it is written, 'The reproaches [or insults] of those who reproached thee fell on me.' " Christ's bearing our reproach showed that He did not please Himself. The "me" in the Romans passage is distinctly Christ, whereas in the psalm, it referred to the psalmist. But both the psalmist and Christ experienced reproach for God. That is the point of comparison. The nature and intensity of the reproach differed, but both were real, historical events.

Other interesting persons are used as types of Christ. One is Solomon in 2 Samuel 7:12–14 and Hebrews 1:5. Or Isaiah in Isaiah 8:16 and Hebrews 2:13. One fascinating study is that of Melchizedek, king of Salem. He is mentioned only twice in the Old Testament and very briefly: Genesis 14:17–20 and Psalm 110:4. But Melchizedek is mentioned in four chapters of Hebrews where he is considered a type of certain aspects of the ministry of Christ, (see Heb. 5:6,10; 6:20; 7:1–11,15–17,21). To the writer of Hebrews, the points of correspondence were Melchizedek's superiority as a priest, his independence from all earthly relations (no mention is made in Genesis of the genealogy of Melchizedek) and the absence of any allusion to his death.

Events Are Used as Types

Events or experiences are sometimes used in typology. A familiar one is the Passover Feast of the Jews. In Exodus 12:21–23, the Israelites were told to kill a lamb and daub blood on the doorposts and tops of their doors so that the death angel would not touch their homes. This was to be commemorated as an annual feast for the Jews. It was the most important feast of the year and some form of the Passover is observed even in our times.

In 1 Corinthians 5:7, Paul wrote, "For Christ, our paschal [passover] lamb, has been sacrificed." The killing of the Passover lamb in the Old Testament depicted metaphorically the death of Christ. The death of the sacrifice is the point of correspondence. The difference lies in the nature of the sacrifice. The superiority of Christ's sacrifice because of who He is and what He did is the theme of Hebrews 9:1—10:18. The life He gave up was an infinite life. The application of meaning to Christ obviously transcends its earlier counterpart.

Both the original Passover and the death of Christ are historical events. Typology gives richer meaning to the Passover and shows the significance of the death of Christ.

Typology also appears in the story of the birth of Jesus

in Matthew 2:17,18. Herod the Great commanded all infants under the age of two to be killed. He hoped to destroy the baby who might become a threat to his political power. In telling the story, Matthew quoted from Jeremiah 31:15:

"A voice was heard in Ramah,
wailing and loud lamentation,
Rachel weeping for her children;
she refused to be consoled,
because they were no more."

In Jeremiah, Rachel, the mother of Joseph and Benjamin (and therefore the "mother" of the northern tribes), weeps for the ten tribes that were carried away to Assyria. Matthew, applying this text to women who lost their infant sons because of Herod's slaughter, is employing typology. The point of correspondence is the grief displayed in the face of terrible tragedy.

Institutions Are Sometimes Types

Sometimes institutions, such as the Temple, were used as types. The Old Testament Temple was a place not only where Jehovah dwelt and was worshiped, but also was a symbol that God was in the midst of His people to strengthen them (see Ps. 68:29,35).

In the New Testament, although the old meaning also occurs, a new, higher application of "temple" is found. In 1 Corinthians 3:16,17, Paul writes: "Do you [plural] not know that you are God's temple and that God's Spirit dwells in you? If any one destroys God's temple, God will destroy him. For God's temple is holy, and that temple you are."

Paul uses the same typology in 2 Corinthians 6:16, "What agreement has the temple of God with idols? For we are the temple of the living God."

The Church of God or the people of God are called

God's temple. This is God's habitation. In Ephesians 2:19–21 Paul speaks of the household of God "built upon the foundation of the apostles and prophets, Christ Jesus himself being the cornerstone, in whom the whole structure is joined together and grows into a holy temple in the Lord; in whom you also are built into it for a dwelling place of God in the Spirit."

The Old Testament priesthood and the nation Israel are used as types of the body of believers. Peter in his first epistle, says: "Like living stones be yourselves built into a spiritual house, to be a holy priesthood, to offer spiritual sacrifices acceptable to God through Jesus Christ. . . . But you are a chosen race, a royal priesthood, a holy nation, God's own people, that you may declare the wonderful deeds of him who called you out of darkness into his marvelous light" (1 Pet. 2:5,9).

The same idea, plus the concept of believers being a "kingdom" appears in Revelation: Jesus Christ "made us a kingdom, priests to his God and Father, to him be glory and dominion for ever and ever" (Rev. 1:6).

"And they sang a new song, saying,
'Worthy art thou to take the scroll
   and to open its seals,
for thou wast slain and by thy blood
   didst ransom men for God
from every tribe and tongue and
   people and nation,
and hast made them a kingdom
   and priests to our God,
and they shall reign on earth' " (Rev. 5:9,10).

"They shall be priests of God and of Christ, and they shall reign with him a thousand years" (Rev. 20:6).

Understanding Typology

1. Note the specific point or points of correspon-

dence between the type and the antitype. These should be examined in the historical context of each.

2. Note the differences and contrasts between the type and the antitype. Seeing the differences helps the interpreter to recognize the true significance of the point or points of correspondence.

3. The New Testament emphasizes the *one people of God*. This emphasis makes typology historical as well as instructional.

Should the student of the Bible feel free to find other "types" in the Old Testament in addition to those used by New Testament writers? There probably are more genuine correspondences than the New Testament writers drew, but certain safeguards should be observed to eliminate sensational and questionable indulgences in typology. *Typology must not become a cover-up for allegorizing.*

1. Be sure the potential type shows a similarity in some *basic* quality or element.

2. Be sure this basic quality or element exhibits God's purpose in the original historical context and also in the historical context of the antitype. God's purpose may not be the same, but the point of correspondence will have the same meaning.

3. Be sure that the lesson gained by typology is also taught in the New Testament by *direct assertion*. This is usually true of the New Testament examples of typology. For example, in Hebrews 1:10–12 the writer quotes Psalms 102:25–27 where God is spoken of as creator and applies it to Christ. However, this typological passage is not the only one that teaches that Christ was involved in creation. Colossians 1:16 says, "For in him [Christ] all things were created, in heaven and on earth ... all things were created through him and for him." John 1:3 asserts the same thing.

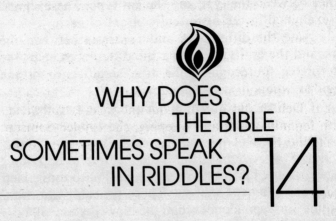

WHY DOES THE BIBLE SOMETIMES SPEAK IN RIDDLES? 14

Some sections of the Bible seem obscure because the historical-cultural background is unfamiliar or because language problems confuse us. A careful study of the history and culture of the times often sheds light on these sections. However, other passages remain difficult even after a thorough study of these factors. In rare instances the original writer may have intended to puzzle his readers!

Riddles in Ancient Times

A riddle is meant to tax the ingenuity of the hearer or reader. Today, riddles are a kind of childhood amusement, but in ancient times, riddles had serious purposes and the destiny of a man or a nation sometimes depended on ability to solve a riddle.

One famous Old Testament riddle is that of Samson in Judges 14:12–20. Samson killed a lion and later was able to get some honey out of the skeleton of the dead beast.

Samson, an Israelite, wanted to marry Delilah, a Philistine. During the extensive feast preceding the wedding, Samson posed a riddle to the 30 "friends of the bridegroom" who had been provided for him by his host as part of the wedding custom:

"Out of the eater came something to eat.

Out of the strong came something sweet" (v. 14).

The 30 men could not guess to what he was referring, and they threatened to burn the house of Delilah's father if Delilah did not find out the answer for them. With feminine wiles and weeping, she cajoled Samson into telling her and then she passed the answer on to the 30 men.

Samson was furious when he found out how they had solved the riddle. A long siege of carnage began that spotlighted the hostility between Israel and the Philistines. In the case of Samson, as in some other instances, a riddle played a devastating part in the history of a nation.

In all biblical riddles, as in Samson's riddle, the student must consider three principles: *the reason* for the riddle; *the content* of the riddle; *the outcome* of the riddle.

One of the most famous riddles appears in Revelation 13:18. Earlier in this chapter John describes the beast from the sea who makes war with the saints. Then he describes the beast from the earth who causes the earth and its inhabitants to worship the first beast. Then comes John's riddle: "Here is wisdom. Whoever has understanding, let him calculate the number of the beast. Now it is the number of a man, and his number is 666" (literal translation).

Many have tried to solve this riddle, but no one can claim he has the solution. By the phrase "number of a man" John meant the numerical value of a man's name. This kind of numerology was well known in ancient times. There were no arabic numerals at that time. Instead, each letter of the Greek and Hebrew alphabets had a numerical value. It was somewhat similar to but much more complex than the Roman numeral system in which V stands for 5; X for 10; and L for 50, etc.

In the Greek system, alpha (A) equals 1, beta (B) equals 2, etc., for the first nine letters; the next nine letters were assigned to the numbers 10, 20, 30, etc.; and the next letters to 100, 200, 300, etc.

The name of Jesus is composed of the Greek letters iota, eta, sigma, omicron, upsilon, and sigma. They have the following numerical values: iota = 10; eta = 8; sigma = 200; omicron = 70; upsilon = 400; sigma = 200. The numerical value of the name of Jesus totaled 888.

John's original readers were those who read Revelation in Greek. There are many combinations of Greek letters that give the total 666, but when the names of known "beasts" or political rulers of the first century are analyzed, the results do not come out to 666.

Prophetic "experts" have been working on this riddle for 1900 years, and they are still doing so. But trying to take English, or Russian, or Italian or Chinese names and figuring out their *Greek* "numerical value" is an exercise in futility and a kind of numbers game. Neither English, nor Italian, nor Russian, nor Chinese nor most other languages have the same alphabet as Greek. Most do not have the same number of letters.

If we try to take names in our time and put them into Greek, we can manipulate a great deal. For example, the English letter "e" could be any one of four Greek letters or diphthongs. The same is true of some consonants. Also, names are spelled differently in different languages. By choosing the spelling he wants and any one of several possible "equivalents" in the Greek language, the prophetic "expert" can get almost any number he desires. This is obviously a misuse of an ancient riddle and should not be taken seriously by the earnest Bible student.

What, then, is the purpose of the riddle? It seems that this "666" riddle is meant to be obscure and ambiguous. The activities, power and influence of the "beast" or Antichrist are much more important than this numerical clue to his name. However, it also seems to indicate that specific persons will play key roles in opposing the people of God.

What do the three principles regarding riddles tell us about this one? *First, the purpose* of the riddle is to focus attention on the Antichrist. *Second, the content* of the riddle uses a common means of designating a person whom the writer did not or could not explicitly name. *Third, the outcome* of the riddle is that the time of the Antichrist's appearance is freed from all specific time settings, since no one in ancient times clearly met the numerical description.

Fables Teach Lessons

A fable is a fictitious story meant to teach a lesson. The characters are often animals, trees, bushes, or plants whose actions, being contrary to their nature, depict the vagaries, emotions, or failure of humans.

Fables have been common in all cultures. In the modern Western world, they are usually considered children's literature, for children readily accept the imagery of animals or trees talking. One familiar fable is that of the wind and the sun vying with each other to see who could make the man take off his coat. The wind tried to blow it off, but the harder he blew, the more tightly the man wrapped the coat around himself. When the sun had his turn and shone warmly on the man, he soon took off his coat.

In Old Testament times, fables were often used by the

prophets. In Judges 9:8–15, Jotham tells the story of trees that once set forth to choose a king. In order of preference, they nominated the olive tree, the fig tree, the vine, and finally the thornbush (bramble or buckthorn). The first three trees declined the nomination because they had more important work to do than "swaying over the trees."

The thorn tree accepted, saying, "If in good faith you are anointing me king over you, then come and take refuge in my shade; but if not, let fire come out of the bramble and devour the cedars of Lebanon" (v. 15).

What pictorial imagery and irony! A thornbush boasting of its shade! A thornbush threatening to set fire to the lofty cedars of Lebanon!

Jotham then applies his fable to Abimelech, who had coerced the people of Shechem to make him king and then hired ruffians to slay his own relatives who might question his right to the throne. After telling the fable, Jotham found it wise to go into exile in Beersheba to escape the wrath of Abimelech.

A very short fable appears in 2 Kings 14:9. Amaziah, king of Judah, had just returned from an impressive victory over the Edomites (2 Kings 14:7). Impressed with himself, and apparently unconcerned about potential loss of life among his men, he sent messengers to Jehoash, king of Israel, announcing that he was about to start war against him for no particular reason except to see which country was the stronger. It was in the spirit of one Little League team challenging another.

Jehoash answered with the short fable. A thistle sent a message to a cedar demanding that the cedar tree give his daughter in marriage to the thistle's son. But before anything could come of the demand, a wild beast trampled down the thistle.

Jehoash applied the fable by suggesting that Amaziah

ought to enjoy his new glory by staying at home. "Why should you provoke trouble so that you fall, you and Judah with you?" (v. 10). The lesson of the fable was plain: human pride can be quickly brushed aside by the relentless events of life.

With this kind of fable (as with other kinds of figurative language) interpreters are tempted to press too far. Some try to make an allegory from this with Amaziah the thistle, Jehoash the cedar and the wild animal the army of Jehoash.

The historical record shows that Amaziah did ignore the lesson of the fable and the advice of Jehoash, made war on Israel and was soundly defeated. But the fable should still be treated as a fable, with its primary lesson that human pride is fragile, easily crushed in life.

Sometimes the Bible combines various kinds of figurative language.

Ezekiel 17:2 states that Ezekiel is to propound a riddle and an allegory, and what follows is essentially a fable, for in it eagles and trees act in ways contrary to their natures. This story is interesting because the application that comes to Ezekiel from the Lord is better understood by us than it was by Ezekiel, for it seems to refer to the coming Messiah and His role in history.

This fable can be divided into three parts: The prophet's riddle and allegory (vv. 1–10); the immediate meaning of the story about the eagles and the vine (vv. 11–21); the final planting of Jehovah when He establishes His Messiah as head over all (vv. 22–24).

The story goes like this: A great eagle comes to Lebanon and crops off the top of the cedar, taking it away to a city of commerce. He takes seed of the land and plants it in surroundings conducive to growth. He plants it as a willow tree is planted and it comes up a low-spreading vine, and its branches turned toward the eagle.

157

However, another eagle comes and the vine turns toward the second eagle. The second eagle transplants the vine to even better soil. The question is then asked, "Will it thrive?" And the answer is "No, it will utterly wither."

In the next section, Ezekiel unfolds the meaning of the story in his day. The first eagle stood for the king of Babylon. The top of the cedar represented Jehoiachin and the princes who were carried away to Babylon. The seed that grew as a low-spreading vine referred to Zedekiah and the people who were left in the land of Israel.

The second eagle, to whom Zedekiah and the people turned, was Egypt. In turning to Egypt, Zedekiah broke his covenant with Nebuchadnezzar that had been confirmed with an oath. In ancient times, solemn statements and affirmations usually invoked the god that a king claimed to serve. In this case, Zedekiah would have called upon his God—Jehovah—as witness to his agreement with Nebuchadnezzar. That is why, in Ezekiel 17:18,19, God pronounced judgment on Zedekiah: "Because he despised the oath and broke the covenant, because he gave his hand and yet did all these things, he shall not escape. . . . As I live, surely my oath which he despised, and my covenant which he broke, I will requite upon his head."

Against this dark background, Ezekiel turns to a brighter picture. The Lord Jehovah will take a young, tender twig (compare Isa. 11:1 and 53:2) from the top of the cedar and plant it on a high and lofty mountain (compare Isa. 2:2–4; Mic. 4:1–5). This tree will bear fruit and be a good cedar.

The reference seems to be to the Messiah. All the birds come and dwell in its branches. All the trees will know that Jehovah has done this. He has brought down the high tree and exalted the low tree. The trees seem

158

to represent nations. The high tree and the green tree stand for those who, at any particular juncture in history, seem to be flourishing. The destiny of individuals and people is controlled by God and is related to their response to the Messiah.

Enigmatic Language in the Bible

Webster defines enigma as "a perplexing statement." Enigmatic statements in the Bible are often perplexing because readers are unprepared for their meaning. Sometimes, today's readers may understand more of the meaning than the original readers because other teachings illuminate the enigmatic portion. Other times, today's readers may understand less than the first readers because the original situation is so distant. Some sayings that were clear in their original setting are now obscure because some elements of the original setting are unknown to us.

Occasionally, a writer states clearly that he knows he is writing enigmatically, but he cannot do otherwise. Some of the reasons for obscurity may be: *the nature of the message itself; the condition of the readers or hearers; the limitations of the writer or speaker.*

In Numbers 12:6–8 the Lord speaks to Aaron and Miriam: "Hear my words: If there is a prophet among you, I the Lord make myself known to him in a vision, I speak with him in a dream. Not so with my servant Moses; he is entrusted with all my house. With him I speak mouth to mouth, clearly, and not in *dark speech*" (italics added).

"Dark speech" is the translation generally given by the *Revised Standard Version* to the Hebrew term that usually refers to enigmatic language. In this passage God says that Moses is in a class by himself in that God speaks to him directly and not by visions, dreams, or

159

dark speech—the means by which He often communicated with His prophets.

The enigmatic language of the Old Testament was not due to the prophets' lack of skill in expressing themselves. It was rather because that was the way God spoke to them. In Psalm 78:2,3 the writer declares:

"I will open my mouth in a parable;
I will utter dark sayings from of old,
things that we have heard and known,
that our fathers have told us."

The psalmist then traces the history of the children of Israel and God's dealing with them.

Not all obscurity is of the same type. When the cause for obscurity is irrevocable—involving the hearer, the message, or the manner in which God spoke—there is no way to clarify.

Sometimes the wise use of the theme of promise and fulfillment sheds some light on the enigmas, but that may not reveal the whole story. The Old Testament as a whole would be an enigma without the New Testament, for there would be promise but no fulfillment. There would be a God who acted in days past but no longer acts. But the Christian with his New Testament has the God who acted in the Old Testament, who acted in Christ and in the Church of Christ's apostles, and who has been active ever since through His Holy Spirit.

We know many of the sayings of Jesus are enigmatic or obscure because of the very controversy that arises over how they should be interpreted. Sometimes what Jesus said was obscure even to His disciples. In John 16:25, Jesus said, "I have said this to you in figures; the hour is coming when I shall no longer speak to you in figures but tell you plainly of the Father."

In John 16:28 Jesus said, "I came from the Father and have come into the world; again, I am leaving the world

160

and going to the Father." His disciples replied, "Ah, now you are speaking plainly, not in any figure!" (v. 29).

Throughout the Gospels there is the implication that neither the crowds nor the disciples really understood what Jesus was saying. When the disciples asked Jesus why He spoke in parables, He answered, "This is why I speak to them in parables, because seeing they do not see, and hearing they do not hear, nor do they understand" (Matt. 13:13). This is followed by three parables dealing with seed-sowing and the response of people to the Word of God.

Concealed or enigmatic language is a reality, but this is no excuse for skipping difficult passages. At the same time it is a warning to anyone who insists that he has *the meaning* that makes further discussion superfluous.

Interpreting Riddles
1. Consider the reason for the riddle.
2. Consider the content of the riddle.
3. Consider the outcome of the riddle.

Interpreting Fables
1. Understand the original situation in which the writer or speaker used the fable.
2. Is the fable simple or complex? Is it teaching a lesson by stressing one point or several points?
3. What was the influence of the fable on its hearers? What was the response of the one who told the fable?
4. Why is the lesson taught in the fable pertinent to people today?

Interpreting Obscure Language
1. Try to get through the superficial ambiguities by checking other translations for possible meanings of words and sentence structures.

2. Pay careful attention to the context so that you can see how the thought flows before, through, and after the obscure portion.

3. Watch for quick shifts from literal to figurative meaning. Where metaphor appears, there is often a sudden shift from literal to figurative meaning. For example, in Luke 11:33–36 Jesus began by saying that a lamp is not put under a bushel basket, but on a lampstand. He then interpreted it metaphorically, "Your eye is the lamp of your body; when your eye is sound [healthy], your whole body is full of light; but when it is not sound, your body is full of darkness."

Thus far the meaning is clear. But the next line is obscure, "Therefore be careful lest the light in you be darkness." Here Jesus seems to have changed to a figurative meaning of the word eye—changing from the physical eye to the "eye" of the soul. The meaning seems to be that when the inward person is sick morally and spiritually, the eye of the soul cannot transmit spiritual light.

The rest of the passage continues in this same vein, "If then your whole body is full of light, having no part dark, it will be wholly bright, as when a lamp with its rays gives you light." This may mean that the amount of light within is like the amount of light outside, when the beam of a lamp completely illuminates the person.

Problems in interpretation often stem from the shifts in literal meaning to metaphorical.

The fourth principle in interpreting obscure language is to *check good commentaries after you have done careful study and thinking for yourself. But be sure to grapple first with the problem yourself.*

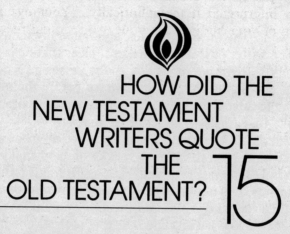

HOW DID THE NEW TESTAMENT WRITERS QUOTE THE OLD TESTAMENT?

15

The careful Bible student who does any independent study soon faces questions about the way New Testament writers quote the Old Testament.

He finds that some Old Testament "quotations" hardly classify as quotations by modern standards. The Old Testament passage in his Bible may be quite different from the way it is quoted by New Testament writers. The reasons are many, but there are three *major* reasons for the differences.

Quotations from the Septuagint

First, the New Testament writer may be quoting from the Septuagint version of the Old Testament. This was the Greek Old Testament, translated from the Hebrew between 250 and 150 B.C. It is the version nearly always used by the New Testament writers who did not know Hebrew, or by those who were writing to Gentile Christians or to Greek-speaking Jewish Christians. This was the only Old Testament that such Christians knew.

For example, Hebrews 1:7 reads, "Of the angels he says, 'Who makes his angels winds, and his servants flames of fire.' "

But the passage in Psalms 104:4 reads, "Who makest the winds thy messengers, fire and flame thy ministers."

The writer of Hebrews makes it clear that he is giving a *highly literal interpretation* to the verses he is quoting from the Septuagint, for the phrase before the quote is "Of the angels he says ..." and uses the quotation to prove that Christ is superior to angels.

Yet the Old Testament reading as we *now* know it (in most modern translations) speaks of God making the winds His messengers and making fire and flame His ministers. It is not discussing angels at all. However, the New Testament writer used the only version his readers knew (the Septuagint) and interpreted that version literally.

Quotations from Memory

Second, the writer may be quoting from memory and not trying to be exact. The New Testament writers did not have a copy of the Old Testament at their fingertips to check each quotation. They wrote under difficult circumstances. Paul wrote from jail cells; others wrote during journeys. How could we expect *exact* quotations?

In Hebrews 2:6,7 the writer indicates that he is quoting from memory, because he says he cannot recall exactly where the passage is found. He wrote: "It has been testified somewhere [he apparently could not remember where],

'What is man that thou art mindful
    of him,
or the son of man, that thou carest
    for him?
Thou didst make him for a little
    while lower than the angels,
thou hast crowned him with glory
    and honor,
putting everything in subjection
    under his feet.' "

This is from Psalm 8:4–6. His memory in verse 4 was nearly perfect. But in verses 5 and 6 there are some differences. The Old Testament passage *(RSV)* reads:

"Yet thou hast made him little less
    than God,
and dost crown him with glory and
    honor.
Thou hast given him dominion over
    the works of thy hands;
thou hast put all things under his feet."

Quotations Altered for Easier Application

Third, sometimes the writer of the New Testament simply altered the original statement to make it adapt more easily to his particular train of thought.

In Ephesians 4:7–12, where the apostle Paul discusses spiritual gifts given to the Church, he quoted from Psalm 68:18. The Ephesians passage reads: "But grace was given to each of us according to the measure of Christ's gift. Therefore it is said, 'When he ascended on high he led a host of captives, and he gave gifts to men.' (In saying 'He ascended,' what does it mean but that he also descended into the lower parts of the earth? He who descended is he who also ascended far above all the heavens, that he might fill all things.) And his gifts were that some should be apostles, some prophets, some evangelists, some pastors and teachers, for the equipment of the saints, for the work of the ministry, for building up the body of Christ."

However, the Old Testament passage uses a figurative picture of a conquering hero returning from battle and *receiving* gifts from men. Psalm 68:17,18: "With mighty chariotry, twice ten thousand, thousands upon thousands, the Lord came from Sinai into the holy place. Thou didst ascend the high mount, leading captives in thy train, and receiving gifts among men, even among the rebellious, that the Lord God may dwell there."

The psalmist is celebrating God's victory.

In the Ephesian passage Paul employs typology. He applies the passage to Christ's victory. By Christ's death and resurrection, He defeated Satan. Believers who formerly were Satan's captives were freed by Christ. Not only have they become free, but Christ has given various gifts to those whom He set free. The gifts are really gifted persons: apostles, prophets, evangelists, pastors and teachers. All these gifts equip the saints to do the work of the ministry.

The lack of preciseness in some Old Testament quotations by New Testament writers is no cause for concern. The New Testament writers used the Old Testament frequently and reverently because they recognized it as God's message to them—a message of authority that demanded their obedience. Their facilities for quoting exactly, and their thought patterns and habits were different from ours—the product of their day. But they shared with saints of all ages their firm belief that God acts, that He has revealed Himself to men, and that men are responsible to God to respond in faith. Fresh applications of God's Word were always important to the writers of the New Testament.

166

Understanding Old Testament Quotations in the New Testament

1. Remember that New Testament writers were quoting from memory, usually *without* the Old Testament scrolls in front of them. Do not expect word for word exactness.

2. Most of the quotations are from the Septuagint, the Greek translation of the Old Testament made about 250 to 150 B.C. By the very nature of translations, we cannot expect the Septuagint translators to give exactly the same translations as our twentieth-century translators, especially since the Hebrew text was written without vowels.

3. The New Testament writers used quotations the way other writers of their day used quotations—not with the exact preciseness demanded by twentieth-century technology. They also adapted them for their purposes.

4. The New Testament writers recognized the authority of the Old Testament—that it was God's Word. That is why they quoted it so frequently.

IS IT
WORTH
THE EFFORT? 16

"Why should the Bible be so complex?" you may be asking. "Why should I need to study history, culture, language problems, non-Western kinds of poetry, and ancient figures of speech to understand God's message to me?"

You don't necessarily have to. You can read the Bible like any other book, in any version you choose, and much of God's message will come through to you if you read with an open mind, seeking the guidance of the Holy Spirit.

Realistically, however, the Bible is NOT like any other book that has ever been written. It involves many writers, spanning many hundreds of years, writing in languages unknown to us, with thought patterns, customs, and historical situations far removed from us.

Even more important, the Bible is not like any other

book because the Bible brings us the *voice of God*. God is far beyond our most profound thoughts, larger than our most emancipated imaginations, more holy than our sinful minds can comprehend, more loving than we have the capacity to experience.

Even the most devoted student will only scratch the surface of the Bible and its revelations of God and God's dealing with man. The Bible speaks about men and women living and dying, of their tragedies, joys, sins, rebellions against God, reconciliations with God. It speaks of Jesus Christ, God's Son, His life and ministry on this earth, His death, resurrection, His present work on behalf of His people.

Because of the very richness of the Bible, we want to be able to absorb and comprehend as much as possible so that we can grow in our love for God, our obedience to Him, our understanding of ourselves and the world in which we live.

There are other reasons why we should be diligent, careful students of the Bible. In our times, sects are multiplying and many are aggressively propagating their beliefs. Most of them make some use of the Bible in approaching prospective converts. They have a well-designed platter of Bible verses that is served up instantly in response to certain questions.

But most of them have little solid knowledge of the Bible—the kind of knowledge based on the principles outlined in this book.

The Christian who knows only a few scattered Bible verses memorized in childhood is hard-pressed to defend his faith in the face of the many kinds of pressures he meets today.

But far more important even than this is the fact that the Bible does not need to be defended; it only needs to be read and understood and applied by the reader. A genuine, solid knowledge of the Bible and how to interpret it frees the Christian from any fears that some new finding can destroy his faith. The truth is not destructible.

Practice Is More Difficult than Theory

To exercise proper care and balance in understanding the Bible is easier to talk about than it is to practice. This is true of most skills. We can read a text on swimming and learn exactly what our arms and legs are supposed to do in the water. We can memorize this information. But that does not mean we will be able to swim when we get into the water. Once in the water we discover that mastering the skill is quite different from memorizing the rules.

It takes time and effort to learn to coordinate elements of biblical interpretation involving language, historical backgrounds, culture patterns, figurative language, etc., to arrive at the original meaning of the passage we are studying and then to determine its rightful meaning for us today. We soon find that understanding the Bible, like swimming, is a personal matter. There is no impersonal way to get at its meaning. There are only guidelines to help persons discover meaning.

It often helps to discuss our findings and methods with fellow Christians from different denominational backgrounds. We may see other views that teach us that our own view is not as absolute as we thought.

If we have already developed bad habits of Bible study, we may feel in the beginning that it is too difficult to change. But there is too much at stake to permit us to take the line of least resistance.

The Holy Spirit will help our honest efforts, reprove our faltering willpower, and help us discipline our thinking as we should.

We Must Account to God for Our Use of the Bible

God has given us the Bible as a means through which we may know Him, and we must account to God for our use of it. Jesus said that people will give account on the day of judgment for every idle and useless word (Matt. 12:36). This surely applies to our use of the Bible.

Sincerity will not be an adequate excuse for poor habits when the real problem is laziness or stubbornness.

How we understand the Bible influences not only our lives but also the lives of many around us. If we are aware that we must give account to God for how we interpet His Word, then we must be honest and diligent in our study of it.

God has given us His Word for our growth and for our witness for Him in the world. He has set us free from the domination and penalty of sin. This Good News must be brought to every man, woman, and child. To do this, we must understand it.

"The unfolding of thy words gives light; it imparts understanding to the simple [inexperienced]" (Ps. 119: 130).

BIBLIOGRAPHY

General Helps for the Bible Student

A. Atlases
The Macmillan Bible Atlas, by Y. Aharoni and M. Avi-Yonah. Macmillan, New York, 1968
Atlas of the Bible, L.H. Grollenberg. Thomas Nelson, New York, 1956
Rand McNally Bible Atlas, E.G. Kraeling. Chicago, 1956

B. Bible Dictionaries
The New Bible Dictionary, J.D. Douglas, et al. Wm. B. Eerdmans, Grand Rapids, Mich., 1962
Pictorial Bible Dictionary, Merrill Tenney. Zondervan Publishing House, Grand Rapids, Michigan, 1963
The New Compact Bible Dictionary, T. Alton Bryant. Zondervan Publishing House, Grand Rapids, Michigan, 1967

C. Bible Commentaries
The New Bible Commentary, Revised, Guthrie, Motyer, Stibbs, Wiseman. Grand Rapids, Mich., Wm. B. Eerdmans, 1970
The Wycliffe Bible Commentary, Pfeiffer and Harrison, Moody Press, Chicago, 1962
The Biblical Expositor, Carl F.H. Henry. A.J. Holman Company, New York, 1973
The Daily Study Bible Series, William Barclay. Westminister Press, Philadelphia. (This is a series of books on the New Testament that is particularly helpful on matters of history and culture of the New Testament period.)

172

INDEX OF
SCRIPTURE PASSAGES
REFERRED TO
OR DISCUSSED